The
McMichael
Canadian Collection

KLEINBURG · ONTARIO

The McMichael Canadian Collection is an agency of the Government of Ontario assisted through the Ministry of Citizenship and Culture.

ACKNOWLEDGEMENTS

Rosemary Shipton	Preface
Bernhard Cinader	Woodland Indian Art
Paul Duval	Biographies
Dorothy Harley Eber	Inuit Art
Howard B. Roloff	West Coast Indian Art
A.J. Casson	Design
Joachim Gauthier	Portraits of Artists
Hugh W. Thompson	Photography
Cook Printing Canada Ltd.	Printer

Revised Edition
© 1983 The McMichael Canadian Collection
ISBN 0-7743-8058-6
Printed in Canada

The McMichael Canadian Collection encompasses more than 2,500 paintings, prints and sculptures, including the largest selection of Group of Seven paintings displayed anywhere. The collection began in 1955 when the founders, Robert and Signe McMichael, purchased Lawren Harris's *Montreal River, Algoma*, followed soon after by Tom Thomson's *Pine Island*. Ten years later the collection had expanded to over 300 works, housed in a large home of hand-hewn logs and native stone built by the McMichaels on the banks of the picturesque Humber River valley at Kleinburg, Ontario. The public, the art community and the surviving members of The Group of Seven showed great interest in the project and in 1965, through the generosity of the McMichaels and the co-operation of the provincial government, the collection and the property were donated to the Province of Ontario. In return, the province assumed responsibility for the safekeeping and maintenance of the art work and grounds.

Under the terms of the gift, Robert and Signe McMichael acted as resident curators of The McMichael Conservation Collection of Art as it was then called, assisted by a small advisory committee. In 1972 Premier William Davis introduced legislation changing the name to The McMichael Canadian Collection, appointing Robert McMichael as Director and making a nine-member Board of Trustees responsible for the affairs of the gallery. Initially, the gallery reported to the Legislature of Ontario through the Minister of Colleges and Universities. This role was later transferred to the Minister of Citizenship and Culture, the Honourable Bruce McCaffrey. In 1981 Robert McMichael resigned the directorship and assumed the new office of Founder Director-Emeritus and Michael Bell was appointed Director and Chief Executive Officer. In 1982 Ian Thom joined the staff as Curator of Collections.

At the time of the 1965 agreement, the collection consisted of about 300 works (roughly half of which had been purchased by the McMichaels; the remainder had been donated), mainly by The Group of Seven, Tom Thomson, Emily Carr, and David Milne. It has since been broadened to realize the McMichaels' vision to include Indian and Inuit prints, sculptures, paintings and masks, as well as works by artists such as Clarence Gagnon, Lionel LeMoine FitzGerald and J.W. Morrice. But the heart of The Collection remains the work of The Group and of Thomson, now numbering more than 1,000 works by Group members and over 80 by Thomson.

As The Collection grew, so did interest in the gallery. Several members of The Group — A.Y. Jackson, A.J. Casson, Edwin Holgate and Frederick Horsman Varley — visited the gallery, as did other Canadian artists including Yvonne McKague Housser, Barker Fairley and Thoreau MacDonald, son of original Group member J.E.H. MacDonald. Casson designed some of the early publications and Thoreau MacDonald did the sketches that illustrate this text. Jackson chose to live with the

McMichaels for the last six years of his life and became a familiar sight moving through the galleries with an admiring group of visitors in tow.

The McMichaels' enthusiasm for the gallery led many people to donate paintings to The Collection and today, about three-fourths of The Collection has been donated. An early donor was Norah de Pencier of Leith, Ontario, who, years before The Group became popular, often invested half her modest salary in Canadian art. Other art patrons and friends of the founders include financier R.A. Laidlaw, who presented twenty-six paintings; C.A.G. Matthews, former employer of both Carmichael and Casson at Sampson Matthews Limited; S. Walter Stewart, who gave thirty Jackson paintings, including *The Red Maple*; automaker R.S. McLaughlin, who donated an important part of his vast art collection; Dr. A.D.A. Mason, friend to several Group members, who gave MacDonald's masterpiece *Leaves in the Brook*; industrialist Percy Hilborn of Preston, who donated Jackson's favourite canvas, *First Snow, Algoma*; and Yvonne McKague Housser, whose late husband Fred wrote a prime reference work on The Group, and who gave paintings by Harris, Jackson, Lismer and Carr. In 1974 the last living member of Thomson's immediate family, his sister Margaret Tweedale, then ninety, donated her entire collection of works by her brother. Two years later, industrialist Garfield Weston, hearing that one of the few large-scale paintings by Tom Thomson in private hands was about to be sold, offered The Collection more than a quarter of a million dollars to purchase it.

Although the paintings in The Collection represent only a small part of The Group's prolific output, many were handpicked by the artists or by people who knew their work well. Lawren Harris, for instance, brought Tom Thomson's work to the attention of Robert Laidlaw, and A.Y. Jackson helped Colonel McLaughlin develop his collection. The library and archives of The Collection contain books, catalogues, photographs and letters by Canadian painters and writers which form an important source of reference material.

The Tom Thomson Shack

The original log and stone home 'Tapawingo' has been expanded many times — twice by the McMichaels and three times by the Province of Ontario — to accommodate the growing collection of paintings and artifacts and the increasing number of visitors. The most significant expansions were the large new wings added by the province in 1967 and 1969 and the huge entrance complex, built in 1973. Despite the massive size of these additions, the original idea was pursued: log and barnwood walls, fieldstone fireplaces, and windows which look out on the woods and fields of the surrounding greenbelt combined to create a unique and appropriate setting for this

Canadian collection. Between 1981 and 1983, the building was renovated to provide a safe facility for the public, improved access for handicapped persons and a safe environment for the art collection.

In 1962, the shack in which Tom Thomson lived and painted in Toronto's Rosedale Ravine, behind The Group's Studio Building was purchased by the founders and moved to the Kleinburg property. It was furnished as Thoreau MacDonald and A.Y. Jackson remembered it from 1915, even to Thomson's easel and palette. Its walls are decorated with reproductions of paintings by members of The Group, and there are copies of a series of witty contemporary caricatures of Group members by Arthur Lismer.

In 1976 the Department of External Affairs and The McMichael Canadian Collection organized a travelling exhibition of forty-four paintings from The Collection. Over the following two years the exhibit was shown in Glasgow, Edinburgh, Aberdeen, London, Hamburg, Bonn, Munich, Oslo and Dublin, and in the Soviet Union at the Hermitage in Leningrad, the Museum of Western and Eastern Art in Kiev, and the Pushkin Museum in Moscow, with catalogues prepared in German, Russian, Norwegian, English and French. International recognition had come for The Collection.

THE GROUP OF SEVEN AND THEIR CONTEMPORARIES

The group of seven artists whose pictures are here exhibited have for several years held a like vision concerning Art in Canada. They are all imbued with the idea that an Art must grow and flower in the land before the country will be a real home for its people.

Group of Seven catalogue, 1920

In May 1920, when The Group of Seven held their first exhibition at the Art Museum of Toronto, they had developed a doctrine of aggressive nationalism and a style of painting derived directly from experience of the Canadian landscape. They expected resistance from critics and collectors alike, and were themselves outspoken opponents of the art establishment — the societies and academies with their elitist, European-dominated ideals.

The artists had come together in the years leading up to the First World War. Tom Thomson, J.E.H. MacDonald, Arthur Lismer, Frederick Varley, Frank Johnston and Franklin Carmichael all worked at one time or another at Grip Limited in Toronto as commercial designers. Often in the evenings they carried their discussions over to the Arts and Letters Club. There they met the financially independent Lawren Harris and launched upon a bold new conception of Canadian art: they would rid themselves of preconceived ideas and paint nature as they found it. In 1913 they invited A.Y. Jackson, whose work they admired, to come from Montreal to join them.

By 1913 their Canadian movement was clearly established, with a definite number of adherents and a common philosophy. In partnership with art patron Dr. James MacCallum, Harris built the Studio Building for Canadian Art overlooking the Rosedale Ravine in Toronto, which assured the artists a home base and studios at a modest cost. Some of them planned a series of sketching trips to Georgian Bay, Algonquin Park and the Laurentians. And, to gain attention and support for their activities, they arranged the 'First Exhibition of Little Pictures by Canadian Artists' at the Toronto Reference Library. Acclaim they achieved, but critiscism too, as one critic branded them 'The Hot Mush School'.

At Thomson's urgings, they continued their sketching trips to the north country. They discovered that the light of the Canadian atmosphere and the shapes and forms of its landscape demanded a new approach to art — one they had seen signalled in the exhibition of contemporary Scandinavian art held at Buffalo in January, 1913. Equipped with specially constructed sketching boxes fitted with standard sized panels, the artists painted from nature, recording the many moods of the wilderness. Some of these sketches they regarded as finished works in themselves, others as preparatory studies for larger canvases to be completed in the studio during the winter. In the fall of 1914, Thomson, Lismer, Jackson and Varley all converged on Algonquin Park, stimulating each other in the intensity of group activity. Jackson and Thomson, working side by side at Oxtongue River, painted their famous *Red Maple* and *Red Leaves* respectively. Thomson gave up full-time employment and for the next three years, working intermittently as a guide, he painted Algonquin Park with exuberant freedom and colour.

War broke out and the group of artists went their separate ways, Jackson and Harris to serve overseas, Varley and others to record events as official war artists. In 1917, Thomson drowned in Canoe Lake. His death shocked his friends, but increased their determination to paint Canada their way. Jackson wrote to MacDonald from France: 'Without Tom the north country seems a desolation of bush and rock, he was the guide, the interpreter, and we the guests partaking of his hospitality so generously given . . . my debt to him is almost that of a new world, the north country, and a true artist's vision.' When they reassembled in 1919 his bereaved colleagues arranged Thomson memorial exhibitions in Montreal, Toronto and Ottawa.

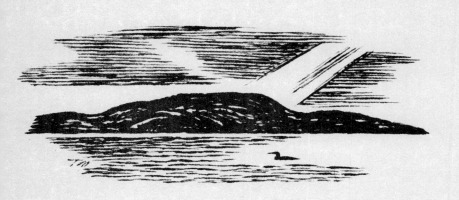

After the war, members of The Group embarked on several sketching trips to the vast Algoma region north of Lake Superior. Harris, MacDonald and Jackson in particular found inspiration here for some of their greatest paintings. Algoma in 1918 was still a wilderness where virtually no one lived and travelling was difficult. The artists moved around by canoe, portaging their tents and art supplies, and thereby enhancing their image as intrepid outdoorsmen. Then Harris had the inspired idea to rent a boxcar from the Algoma Central Railway and have it shunted onto sidings near choice painting locations. His letter to MacDonald indicates the excitement they felt: 'Well James, Me boy, down on your knees and give great gobs of thanks to Allah!...we have a car waiting us on the Algoma Central!!! A car to live in, eat in and work out of. They will move us about as we desire and leave us on auspicious sidings that we may proceed to biff the landscape into a cocked hat at our sweet will...' In September, 1918, Harris, MacDonald, Frank Johnston and Dr. MacCallum made the first boxcar trip. The following year Jackson replaced MacCallum. During this second trip Jackson painted the sketch for *First*

Snow, Algoma, and MacDonald the sketches for *Leaves in the Brook, Algoma Waterfall*, and *Forest Wilderness*. The canvases from these sketches (and the sketch for *Leaves in the Brook*) are now in The McMichael Canadian Collection.

It was after this trip that the Studio Building friends decided to organize The Group of Seven and to hold their first exhibition at the Art Museum of Toronto. Undoubtedly, if the war had not intervened, The Group would have been formed some years earlier and would have included Thomson. The 1920 show, along with the statement of belief published in the catalogue, marked The Group as a vital movement in Canadian art. The timing was opportune, for there was a growing acceptance that Canadian art must be Canadian in inspiration, and both the Ontario government and the newly reorganized National Gallery had supported Group painters with encouragement and with purchases since 1913. Press reaction to the 1920 exhibit was gently encouraging, though several major critics chose to ignore it.

Further exhibitions at the Art Gallery in 1921, 1922, 1925, 1926, 1930 and 1931, and innumerable small showings in towns and cities across the country, drew increasing comment and acceptance. In 1923, however, when the National Gallery and the Royal Canadian Academy clashed over whose responsibility it was to choose Canadian entrants for the 1924 British Empire Exhibition at Wembley, The Group of Seven was caught in the crossfire. Hector Charlesworth of *Saturday Night* accused The Group of instituting a 'cult of ugliness,' while Barker Fairley in the *Canadian Forum* and Bess Housser in the *Canadian Bookman* rose to the defence of The Group. When at the conclusion of the exhibition the Tate Gallery purchased only one Canadian painting, Jackson's *Entrance to Halifax Harbour*, The Group seemed vindicated. A triumphant National Gallery published the almost unanimous praise of the British critics 'to show the very great interest and high opinion of Canadian art held abroad.'

By 1926, when Fred Housser published *A Canadian Art Movement: The Story of The Group of Seven*, the 'young rebels' had attained a critical and public acceptance which established them as the 'National School'.

In the mid-twenties, members of The Group increasingly dispersed. Jackson visited Quebec to paint after an absence of almost eight years, Harris and MacDonald travelled to Nova Scotia and Harris and Jackson went off to the north shore of Lake Superior. This new land obviously made a deep impression on all the artists. Harris returned to Lake Superior every fall for the next three years; MacDonald, Jackson, Varley, Lismer and Harris found opportunities over the next decade to travel to western Canada; and in 1927 Jackson, accompanied by Frederick Banting, was the first Group member to visit the Arctic, repeating the trip three years later accompanied by Harris. Varley accepted a position at the Vancouver School of Art; MacDonald became principal of the Ontario College of Art; and Lismer, first at an art college in Nova Scotia, then at the Ontario College of Art, the Art Gallery of Toronto and the Montreal Museum of Fine Arts, became renowned as a great teacher. Harris joined the Theosophical Society, convinced that art must express spiritual values in addition to portraying the visible world.

The Group of Seven had become an institution, wielding a national influence. 'The prejudice against the Group is pretty well dying out...' Jackson commented in 1930, 'Today, practically all the younger artists are working along the lines we followed.' The organization of the Group remained loose, however. Members met formally only once or twice a year to discuss forthcoming exhibitions, possible trips and the admission of new members. Frank Johnston resigned in 1922 and A.J. Casson, Edwin Holgate and Lionel LeMoine FitzGerald were added in 1926, 1931 and 1932, respectively.

After the final exhibition in December, 1931 and MacDonald's death the following year, The Group disbanded to make way for the formation of a more broadly based group called The Canadian Group of Painters. In the catalogue to its first exhibition in 1933 it proudly claimed to be a direct outgrowth of The Group of Seven. It drew its members from all

across Canada, was open to men and women alike and was concerned with the full range of artistic expression — figure, landscape and abstract paintings. While many excellent artists exhibited through the Canadian Group in the next thirty-six years, including Emily Carr and David Milne, it never achieved the camaraderie, the group spirit, of the original Seven.

The wealth of Canadian art treasures that forms The McMichael Canadian Collection is due largely to those who have generously given their cherished works of art. They were willing to share these with all Canadians and, in so doing, have placed this wider interest above their own personal pride and pleasure of ownership. They will be held in the highest esteem by this and future generations.

DONORS TO THE McMICHAEL CANADIAN COLLECTION

Alcan Canada Products Limited
Dr. F.J. Argue
H.J. Ariss
E. Caven Atkins
C.S. Band
Lady Banting
André Biéler
B.C. Binning
Mrs. J.M. Bishop
Molly Bobak
Ruth E. Bond
Arthur Bourinot
Mrs. J.M. Bowman
Mr. A. Bray
Katherine Brett
Marjorie Lismer Bridges
Mrs. G.E. Britton
Mr. Victor Brooker
Frank Erichsen Brown
Mr. & Mrs. K.J. Butler
Mr. & Mrs. Allan Buxton
G. Caiserman-Roth
Mrs. Hugh Cameron
Mrs. J.H. Cameron
Mr. & Mrs. H.J. Campbell
Canada Packers Limited
Canada Permanent Trust Company
Canadian Imperial Bank of Commerce
Mr. & Mrs. W.J.P. Cannon
Mr. D.G. Carmichael
Mr. A.J. Casson
City of Toronto
Paraskeva Clark
Mr. & Mrs. H. Spencer Clarke
Mrs. R. Colerick
Rogers G. Colgrove
Mrs. J.E. Collins
Mr. C.F. Comfort
Robert H. Cooke Estate
Mr. & Mrs. Rody Kenny Courtice
Crown Life Insurance Company
Mr. H.S. Croxford
Kathleen Daly
Mr. & Mrs. C.W. Densmore
Norah de Pencier
Mrs. E.C. Dixon
Miss Irene Doole
Mr. & Mrs. R.E. Dowsett
Douglas M. Duncan Bequest
Dr. Norman Epstein
William Evans
Fairview Mall Merchants Association
Mrs. G.B. Ferguson
Mrs. Patti Fleury

Mr. Stephen H. Freedhoff
Mr. W.E. Gale
Mrs. G.C. Gardiner
Mr. & Mrs. Arthur B. Gill
Dr. & Mrs. Allan Gonor
James Gordaneer
Harold Groves
Dr. & Mrs. Walton Groves
Mr. Donald Guthrie
Norman Hallendy
Mrs. Chester Harris
Howard K. Harris Bequest
Mrs. Lawren Harris
Mr. & Mrs. L.P. Harris
Donald S. Harvie
Mrs. B. Cogill Haworth
Peter Haworth
Mr. G. Henry
Percy R. Hilborn
Syd Hoare
Mrs. J.D. Holbrook
Mr. Edwin Holgate
Yvonne McKague Housser
Mrs. Alma Houston
Sophia Hungerford
Inco Limited
Mr. A.Y. Jackson
Mr. & Mrs. J.A. Jackson
Henry Wanton Jones
Dr. Wallace Joyce
Mr. Edward J. Kernaghan
Walter Kinsman Estate
Mr. & Mrs. Walter Klinkhoff
John Korner
Mr. & Mrs. T.V. Kristiansen
Mr. R.A. Laidlaw
Patrick Landsley
A.J. Latner Family
Mary Jane Myrtle Leslie Bequest
A.H. Libby
Miss Mabel Lockerby
Mrs. B.E. MacDonald
Jack S. MacDonald
Thoreau MacDonald
Mr. & Mrs. Keith MacIver
Manufacturers Life Insurance Company
Mr. & Mrs. R.W.M. Manuge
Dr. Arnold Mason
Hart Massey
Mr. & Mrs. R.G. Mastin
Mr. C.A.G. Matthews
Mr. D.G. Matthews
Mr. L.R.H. Matthews
McGregor Young Estate

Miss Anne McAughtrie
Mrs. W.E. McGillivray
Mrs. B.K. McIlwraith
Miss Jean McIsaac
Col. R.S. McLaughlin
Miss I. McLaughlin
Mr. & Mrs. R. McMichael
Hon. J.C. McRuer
Miss Grace Melvin
Mrs. Edwin Meredith
Mr. Herbert Merry
Mr. Alexander Millar
Leo Mol
Mrs. J.R. Mooney
Mrs. Kathleen Morris
Mr. Robert Morrison
Mrs. H.L. Morrison
Mr. Ross Murray
Mr. J.A. Newell
David E. Newman
Mrs. Jean Newman
Dr. D.N. Nicolson
W.A. Norfolk
Will A. Ogilvie
Olivetti Canada Limited
Toni Onley
Oshawa Y.W.C.A.
Sir L. Outerbridge
Mr. Herb Palmer
Dr. Jack Parnell
Mr. & Mrs. W.D. Patterson
Mr. N.A. Pelletier
Pepsi-Cola Canada Limited
Philips Electronics Industries Limited
Mr. Roger Pierce
Mr. & Mrs. R. Pope
Mr. D.S. Porter
Miss Claire Pratt
Mrs. E.J. Pratt
Mr. J.J. Rankin
Dr. Benjamin Raxlen
Dr. Samuel Raxlen
Dr. J.K. Reynolds
Goodridge Roberts
Mrs. F.E. Robson
Mr. Howard B. Roloff
Mrs. H.L. Rous
Royal Bank of Canada
Mr. T.P. Ryan
Miss A. Saltmarsh
Mr. Sam Sarick
Anne Douglas Savage
Carl Schaefer
Mr. & Mrs. F. Schaeffer

Jean Scott
Mrs. Marion Scott
Janet Senior
L. Sessenwein
Jack L. Shadbolt
Shell Canada Limited
Shulton of Canada Limited
Herbert Siebner
Mrs. Phillip Sims
M. Sloan
Dr. & Mrs. Robert E. Smart
Gordon Smith
Blanche Snell Bequest
Mr. & Mrs. N. Socha
Dr. and Mrs. J. Murray Speirs
Mrs. Geraldine Staples
Mrs. Tobie Steinhouse
Dr. & Mrs. Max Stern
Frances R. Stevens
Mr. S. Walter Stewart
Mrs. D. Stone
Studio City, Kleinburg
Mr. H. Sutherland
J. Sherwood Taylor
Mr. J.G. Thompson
Maj. F.A. Tilston
Toronto Dominion Bank
The Toronto Star
Margaret Thomson Tweedale
Dr. Walter Unger
Union Carbide Canada Limited
University of Toronto, School of Nursing
Dr. & Mrs. R.W.I. Urquhart
Mr. A. Vanderstarp
Mr. & Mrs. J.J. Vaughan
Mrs. Eleanor Wagner
Sydney H. Watson
Mr. R.C. Webb
Gustav Weisman
Mrs. C.A. Wells
W. Garfield Weston Foundation
Miss D.E. Williams
Mr. & Mrs. D.F. Williams
Duffy Wilson
York Wilson
Wintario
Mr. C.F. Wood
Xerox of Canada Limited
Miss Nina Yeomans
York Memorial Collegiate Institute
Mr. J.D. Young
Mr. N.D. Young
and others

TOM THOMSON 1877-1917

The life of Tom Thomson was the pure stuff of legends. Most of his later years were lived alone in the forest. His early death, in mysterious circumstances, plus the meteor-like briefness of his dazzling career, combined to turn him into a national icon of art.

Tom Thomson's art has always had a special meaning for Bob and Signe McMichael, as it has for most Canadians. The magic of his style, his close identification with the wilderness and his legendary career have put him to the forefront of an art that is truly Canadian. The name of Tom Thomson is synonymous with the search for a native art expression. The magnificent selection of his work in the McMichael Canadian Collection allows one to see his search through its total evolution.

Although he was not yet forty when he drowned in Algonquin Park's Canoe Lake, Thomson achieved an astonishing body of work. His large canvases are few, but his small oil panels number into hundreds. He managed to produce these while spending much of his time as a guide and forest ranger.

Thomson's finest and most characteristic art was compressed into a brief period of three years, from 1914 until his death in the summer of 1917. Thomson started very slowly as an artist. He was doing dull, imitative, and not very accomplished drawings of figures and landscapes well into his thirties, an age when most artists have already achieved a personal authority of style. In the McMichael Collection examples of these early founderings are available to provide valuable comparisons with the achievements of his last years. It is difficult to believe that these earlier pieces were done only a few years before Thomson first visited Algonquin Park and became, virtually overnight, a totally equipped landscape painter.

In the little *Fairy Lake* sketch of 1910, Thomson gives some inkling of his ability to capture mood, but it is still a painting dictated by the subject: the artist is not in full command. In the canvas *Afternoon, Algonquin Park,* Thomson begins to find his true style — that combination of exact observation and spirited execution that was his own. Then in such 1915 sketches as *Burned Over Land* and *The Log Flume,* he breaks into the radiant colour and commanding brushwork that led to the climactic intensity of his last 1917 studies.

The McMichael Canadian Collection exhibits many of Thomson's most masterly late sketches. It would be difficult to imagine more spirited and compelling landscapes than these small masterpieces. From the pictorial resources of Algonquin Park, Thomson mined such glowing compositions as *Autumn Birches, Tea Lake Dam, Tamaracks, Ragged Pine* and *Autumn Colour,* all painted in 1915 and 1916. These on-the-spot sketches were the work of a few hours at most, but they will survive as long as a love for Canadian art survives.

Born in Claremont, Ontario, in 1877, Tom Thomson spent his boyhood in Leith, near Owen Sound. He wandered briefly to Seattle, Washington, then settled in Toronto as a commercial artist, but finally found his spiritual and creative home in Algonquin Park. Today, in the McMichael Canadian Collection and its natural surroundings, with his shack close by, Tom Thomson has found a different sort of home, where millions in the future will be able to see our land through his eyes.

In tribute to Thomson, it would be difficult to improve on J.E.H. MacDonald's description of him, written for a memorial cairn in Algonquin Park: "He lived humbly but passionately with the wild. It made him brother to all untamed things of nature. It drew him apart and revealed itself wonderfully to him. It sent him out from the woods only to show these revelations through his art. And it took him to itself at last."

◄ **Summer Shore, Georgian Bay.** c. 1916
71.5 x 76.3 cm.
1977.31

Sunrise. 1915
21.6 x 26.7 cm.
1966.16.72

Afternoon Algonquin Park. c. 1914
63.2 x 81.1 cm.
1966.16.76

Sombre Day. c. 1916
21.5 x 26.7 cm.
1966.15.21

Snow Shadows. c. 1915
21.2 x 26.7 cm.
1968.18

Spring Break-up. 1916
21.6 x 26.7 cm.
1981.78.2

Pine Cleft Rocks. 1915
21.1 x 26.7 cm.
1971.11

Autumn, Algonquin Park. c. 1915
51.8 x 41.0 cm.
1975.22

Snow in the Woods. c. 1916
21.8 x 27.2 cm.
1981.78.1

TOM THOMSON

TOM THOMSON

Phantom Tent. c. 1915
21.2 x 26.7 cm.
1969.2.3

TOM THOMSON

Moonlight and Birches. c. 1916
22.0 x 27.0 cm.
1966.2.5

Spring Flood. c. 1915
21.2 x 26.7 cm.
1966.15.23

Autumn Birches. c. 1916
21.6 x 26.7 cm.
1966.2.3

Spring. 1914
22.2 x 26.7 cm.
1972.5.4

Algonquin Waterfall. c. 1916
21.2 x 26.7 cm.
1972.4

Wood Interior, Winter. c. 1915
21.9 x 26.7 cm.
1974.9.3

Rocks and Deep Water. 1916
21.1 x 26.5 cm.
1966.16.74

Black Spruce in Autumn. c. 1916
21.5 x 26.8 cm.
1966.14

TOM THOMSON

TOM THOMSON

Beech Grove. c. 1915
21.7 x 26.5 cm.
1966.16.71

Windy Day. c. 1916
21.5 x 26.6 cm.
1966.15.19

New Life After Fire. c. 1914
21.5 x 26.7 cm.
1969.1

Tamaracks. c. 1916
21.4 x 26.8 cm.
1968.12

TOM THOMSON

Aura Lee Lake. c. 1915
21.3 x 26.7 cm.
1970.2

Pine Island. c. 1914
21.7 x 26.7 cm.
1966.16.70

The Log Flume. 1915
21.5 x 26.7 cm.
1969.13.3

Islands, Canoe Lake. 1916
21.2 x 26.7 cm.
1966.16.73

Backwater. 1915
21.5 x 26.7 cm.
1981.39

Algonquin, October. c. 1915
26.8 x 21.6 cm.
1966.16.68

Summer Day. c. 1915
21.6 x 26.8 cm.
1966.15.18

A. Y. JACKSON

First Snow, Algoma. c. 1920
107.4 x 127.7 cm.
1966.7

A.Y. JACKSON 1882-1974

The name of A.Y. Jackson has been more closely associated with the McMichael Canadian Collection than that of any other artist. Jackson encouraged and supported the creation of the Collection from its beginnings and helped formulate its early character. It was ideally fitting that, after a lifetime of travel he chose to spend his last years as an artist-in-residence at the Kleinburg gallery. There, he was available to meet and advise any of the interested public about the Group of Seven and their contemporaries. For thousands of visitors — especially schoolchildren — to the Collection, "A.Y." was a warm link with a heroic creative period of Canada's past.

The artistic Odyssey of A.Y. Jackson began in Montreal, where he studied as a young man under William Brymner, who also taught fellow Group member, Edwin Holgate. After studying and painting in Europe, he was encouraged by Lawren Harris and J.E.H. MacDonald to settle in Toronto in 1913. The next year, he took up residence with other future members of the Group of Seven in the famous Studio Building in Toronto's Rosedale Valley. Jackson remained at the Studio Building for most of his life, using it as a base from which he sojourned in his countless painting trips that covered the breadth of Canada.

Over a career of more than six decades, Jackson came to know the geographic features of this country better than any other man. He came to know it intimately from the vantage point of his sketch box, from Newfoundland to the Pacific and into the farthest recesses of the Arctic. During his wanderings, he did not forget the presence of man at the edge of the wilderness. He affectionately portrayed Quebec's pastel-hued rural villages, Ontario's northern mining towns, ice-bound Eskimo settlements and British Columbia's Indian enclaves.

Jackson's art forms a visual diary proclaiming pictorial paeans to the physical shape of his homeland. From its pages emerge the bleak Arctic tundras, the glories of Algoma autumns, the gently swelling forms of the Prairies, the rolling hills of the Laurentians, the ice-blue features of the Polar icecaps and the thrusting challenge of the Rockies. As an artist, Jackson was of necessity often a loner, but he took an infectious enjoyment in his fellow men. Wherever he went, he made new friends and admirers until, in the end, he became in the minds of most of his countrymen, the living symbol of Canadian art. In a more specific way, Jackson used his enormous energy and experience to teach and lecture between his painting journeys.

The more than 150 works in the McMichael Canadian Collection present an unrivalled survey of A.Y. Jackson's art from its beginnings. Here are to be seen all of the gradual stylistic progressions that marked his career from the delicate water-colour, *Elms and Wildflowers* of 1902, to drawings of Newfoundland executed half a century later. Among his oils done early in this century are the subtle impressionist panel of *Venice*, 1913 and the canvas *Sand Dunes, Etaples* of 1912. From this same formative period, the McMichael Canadian Collection includes some unexpected subjects by Jackson. *The Parlour* of 1910 is an interior study of Jackson's aunt's home in Berlin, Ontario, now Kitchener. In the background of this painting may be seen the Dutch masterpiece, *Incredulity of St. Thomas*, by the seventeenth-century artist, Hendrick Terbrugghen, which now hangs in the Rijksmuseum in Amsterdam. Two other unusual early compositions are a still life of *Dahlias* and *Figure Against the Sky*, both painted in 1913. From that period on, with the exception of the witty self-portrait *Père Raquette*, Jackson appears in the Collection as the great painter of the Canadian landscape so familiar to every Canadian.

Barns. c. 1926
21.6 x 26.8 cm.
1966.5.4

Sunlit Tapestry. c. 1939
71.5 x 91.6 cm.
1966.16.98

Valley of Gouffre River. 1933
64.0 x 81.8 cm.
1968.20

Winter Morning, St. Tite des Caps. 1937
54.0 x 66.5 cm.
1968.24

Fishing Boats on Gaspe Shore. 1934
26.8 x 34.3 cm.
1969.7.5

Quebec Village. c. 1930
21.4 x 26.7 cm.
1966.16.102

Eskimos and Tent. c. 1927
21.5 x 26.8 cm.
1968.8.7

Grey Day, Laurentians. c. 1933
54.0 x 66.2 cm.
1966.2.6

Indian Home. c. 1926
21.1 x 26.6 cm.
1968.8.3

Skeena Crossing, B.C. (Gitsegyukla). c. 1926
53.5 x 66.1 cm.
1968.8.27

Père Raquette. c. 1921
80.0 x 64.5 cm.
1968.8.25R

The Red Maple. 1914
21.6 x 26.9 cm.
1968.8.18

Iceberg at Godhaven. 1930
21.1 x 26.7 cm.
1968.8.15

Lake in the Hills. c. 1922
63.5 x 81.5 cm.
1968.9

Nellie Lake. c. 1933
77.0 x 81.0 cm.
1968.8.28

A. Y. JACKSON

Sand Dunes, Etaples, France. c. 1912
54.6 x 64.8 cm.
1968.11

Cathedral at Ypres. c. 1917
21.7 x 26.8 cm.
1968.8.10

Venice. 1913
21.3 x 26.2 cm.
1968.8.9

October, Lake Superior. 1923
21.2 x 26.6 cm.
1968.8.21

Algoma, November. c. 1924
26.6 x 34.8 cm.
1966.16.99

A. Y. JACKSON

Above Lake Superior. 1924
117.0 x 148.0 cm.
1968.8.26

The Parlour. 1910
36.0 x 41.1 cm.
1972.18.3

Superstition Island, Great Bear Lake. c. 1950
53.3 x 66.0 cm.
1968.25.6

Houses, St. Urbain. c. 1934
21.8 x 26.8 cm.
1981.21

A. Y. JACKSON

A.Y.JACKSON.

River, St. Urbain. 1943
21.2 x 26.8 cm.
1981.37

Alberta Foothills. 1937
64.0 x 81.2 cm.
1971.13.8

Church at St. Urbain. 1931
53.8 x 66.2 cm.
1968.8.29

J. E. H. MacDONALD

Algoma Waterfall. 1920
76.3 x 88.5 cm.
1968.7.2

J.E.H. MACDONALD 1873-1932

No Canadian landscape painter possessed a richer command of colour and pigment than J.E.H. MacDonald. His finest achievements weave together glowing pigment, brushwork and design into tapestry-like compositions. The best of these are now familiar touchstones of Canadian culture.

MacDonald was known to his fellow-artists as a gentle, reserved man, yet his paintings are among the most powerful by the Group of Seven and present the most commanding orchestrations of colour. MacDonald could merge surprising combinations of oranges, reds, greens and violets together with dramatic and controlled effect. His early skills as a draughts-man enabled him to join brilliant drawing to his singular colour sense. His actual brushwork is at once disciplined and vigorous. His best on-the-spot sketches possess an intensity and freshness of execution not dissimilar from Van Gogh.

MacDonald began his career as a commercial designer and in that capacity met Tom Thomson and encouraged the younger artist to paint landscapes. MacDonald was undoubtedly the biggest single influence upon Thomson. From his earliest years, MacDonald was a natural teacher, eager to share his knowledge, enthusiasm and experience. Many painters bene-fited from his instruction and the last ten years of his life were devoted to teaching at the Ontario College of Art. He was principal of the College when he died in 1932.

In 1909, MacDonald was one of the first to paint in Northern Ontario. His early impressions of that period are muted, almost monochrome studies. In the following years, he was laying the disciplined groundwork for such blazing out-bursts of colour as *The Tangled Garden* of 1916, a *tour de force* of hue and texture that represented a revolution in Canadian painting. MacDonald usually reserved his rebel statements to paint itself, a medium which he knew could speak more eloquently for him than words. When MacDonald did write for publication, it was usually lyric poetry and a number of these were collected together in the volume *West By East*, illustrated by his son, Thoreau.

MacDonald travelled less frequently than many other members of the Group of Seven. His obligations as a com-mercial artist and later as a teacher limited his sketching journeys. Of all the places he did visit, the Algoma area of Northern Ontario inspired him the most. What Mont Ste. Victoire was to Cézanne or Arles to Van Gogh, Algoma was to MacDonald. It represented for him a landscape talisman that brought forth his most complete creative response. In Algoma, his art reached its zenith. In brief trips to the area in 1918 and 1919, he amassed the brilliant sketches from which he composed such unforgettable masterpieces as *The Solemn Land, Leaves In The Brook, Autumn In Algoma, Falls On The Montreal River, Algoma Waterfall* and *Forest Wilderness*.

In the McMichael Canadian Collection, MacDonald is represented by several famous canvases and a superb selection of his oil sketches, on panel. Among his major works on view are the great close-up composition, *Leaves In The Brook* and the magnificent, panoramic *Forest Wilderness*, originally in the R.S. McLaughlin Collection. These two works compare in textural and chromatic richness to *Algoma Waterfall*, painted at the same period. The later, more restrained, mountain phase of MacDonald's art is well represented by *Goat Range, Rocky Mountains*, of 1932. MacDonald's small, on-the-spot sketches rival Thomson's in their variety, richness of colour and technical dexterity. Each one of these marvelous small creations is a complete painting in itself. Although many served as models for later studio canvases, MacDonald clearly con-sidered his sketches totally realized impressions at the time of their execution.

Buckwheat Field. c. 1923
21.4 x 26.5 cm.
1966.16.33

Lodge Interior, Lake O'Hara. c. 1925
21.4 x 26.6 cm.
1966.16.36

Artist's Home and Orchard. 1927
21.5 x 26.4 cm.
1969.3

J. E. H. MacDONALD

Silver Swamp, Algoma. 1919
21.4 x 26.6 cm.
1972.18.4

Northern Lights. c. 1916
20.2 x 25.4 cm.
1966.16.41

Aurora, Georgian Bay. 1931
21.5 x 26.7 cm.
1966.15.13

Forest Wilderness. 1921
122.0 x 152.0 cm.
1968.7.1

J. E. H. MacDONALD

Autumn, Algoma. 1920
21.4 x 26.7 cm.
1966.15.5

Beaver Dam and Birches. c. 1919
21.5 x 26.5 cm.
1966.16.49

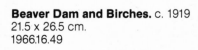

Algoma Forest. 1919
21.4 x 26.5 cm.
1966.15.7

J. E. H. MacDONALD

Wild Ducks. c. 1916
20.2 x 25.4 cm.
1966.16.42

Lichen Covered Shale Slabs. 1930
21.4 x 26.6 cm.
1969.7.3

Agawa Canyon. c. 1920
21.3 x 26.6 cm.
1966.16.48

Young Maples, Algoma. 1918
21.6 x 26.7 cm.
1966.16.31

J. E. H. MacDONALD

Mountain Stream. 1930
21.4 x 26.6 cm.
1966.15.11

Moose Lake, Algoma. 1920
21.3 x 26.5 cm.
1966.15.4

Cathedral Peak, Lake O'Hara. 1927
21.4 x 26.6 cm.
1966.15.9

J. E. H. MacDONALD

Goat Range, Rocky Mountains. 1932
53.8 x 66.0 cm.
1979.35

J. E. H. MacDONALD

Icebergs, Davis Strait. 1930
121.9 x 152.4 cm.
1971.17

LAWREN HARRIS

1885-1970

Lawren Harris was the prime leader of Canadian art for many decades. He was the main force that brought together and joined the varying talents and temperaments which formed the Group of Seven. For many years after the disbanding of the Seven, he remained a powerful force in Canadian painting, aiding and encouraging Emily Carr and a host of younger artists. He was also a founder of the now famous Canadian Group of Painters, which succeeded the Group of Seven in 1933.

Harris was a constant experimenter. He did not hesitate to launch into a new style when he was convinced that he had completely explored the one preceding. No painter of his country approached the variety of pictorial expression commanded by Harris. Throughout a long lifetime of searching, his work passed through five major periods ranging from the impressionistic Toronto "house" paintings of the early 1900s, through richly pigmented, tapestry-like landscapes of Algoma, dramatically designed compositions of the North Shore of Lake Superior, the blue and white crystal-like compositions of the Arctic and the Rockies, to his last phase of total abstraction.

Born in Brantford, Ontario, in 1885, Harris's career took him to Toronto, Massachusetts, New Mexico and Vancouver; but wherever he went Harris held firm to his dedication to the native Canadian outlook he first stated in the catalogue of the 1920 Group of Seven exhibition: "The group of seven artists whose pictures are here exhibited have for several years held a like vision concerning art in Canada. They are all imbued with the idea that an art must grow and flower in the land before the country will be a real home for its people."

Harris's paintings have indeed helped make Canada a real spiritual home for millions of its people. His vision was primed for the far horizons of his own country, and he had need to nurture his eyes on its open spaces. He made several trips to Europe, but each time he returned home complaining that "everything was too close." He recognized the supreme traditions of European art, but his own pressing desire was to create something individual and fresh. In his finest works he achieved that goal magnificently.

It would be difficult to visualize a richer representation of Lawren Harris's varied styles than can be seen in the McMichael Canadian Collection. His career began with a series of almost sombre landscapes painted in 1910 and 1911, mostly of the environs of Toronto. These undistinguished early efforts were followed by works done on trips to the Laurentians, Algonquin Park and Georgian Bay in 1912, when he emerged as a painter with a developing style of his own. The resonant gold and brown Laurentian studies is typified in the Collection by *Laurentians* 1912. From the same year come his *Algonquin Park Sunburst* and *Old Houses Toronto*. In the years between 1912 and 1920, Harris portrayed his houses and landscapes in heavy tapestry-like paint textures. Among the brilliant sketches from this period on view are *Algoma Woodland* 1919, *Beaver Dam* 1919, *Montreal River* 1920 and *Red Maples* 1920.

Of Harris's monumental blue and white phase which began in the early 1920s, the Collection owns many masterpieces, including *Pic Island* 1923, *Lake Superior Island* c. 1923, *Mt. Lefroy* 1930, *Mountains and Lake* 1929 and *Lake and Mountains* 1927. The superb Arctic paintings of 1930 include *Eclipse Sound, Bylot Island, Ellesmere Island* and the monumental *Icebergs, Davis Strait*. These Arctic works of 1930-31 seem an inevitable extension of his Lake Superior and Rocky Mountain experiences. From unpopulated lands of rock he moved into a scene even more remote where there was almost no land, only floating ice and sky and water.

The Arctic voyage and the pictures resulting from it virtually brought Harris's career as a landscape painter to a close and ushered in his period of non-objective art.

Mt. Lefroy. 1930
133.5 x 153.5 cm.
1975.7

LAWREN HARRIS

Northern Lake. c. 1923
82.5 x 102.8 cm.
1968.7.5

Snow, Rocky Mountains. c. 1925
26.8 x 35.3 cm.
1969.13.1

Country North of Lake Superior #2. c. 1921
26.0 x 35.0 cm.
1974.11.1

Algoma Canyon. c. 1923
30.1 x 37.8 cm.
1968.16.3

Shimmering Water, Algonquin Park. 1922
82.3 x 102.0 cm.
1966.16.87

Newfoundland Coast. c. 1921
26.8 x 34.9 cm.
1968.16.2

Lake Superior Cliffs. c. 1921
30.2 x 38.0 cm.
1966.16.84

Mountains and Lake. 1929
91.9 x 114.8 cm.
1970.1.1

Eclipse Sound, Bylot Island. 1930
30.2 x 38.0 cm.
1968.7.3

Algoma Reflections. c. 1919
27.0 x 35.1 cm.
1978.34.2

South End of Maligne Lake. c. 1925
27.0 x 35.2 cm.
1968.16.1

Little House. c. 1911
19.9 x 14.2 cm.
1966.15.30

Lake and Mountains. 1927
30.3 x 38.0 cm.
1972.18.12

Lake Superior Island. c. 1923
74.2 x 89.0 cm.
1966.5.3

Mount Temple. c. 1924
30.5 x 38.1 cm.
1968.25.11

ARTHUR LISMER 1885-1969

Arthur Lismer was the great teacher of the Group of Seven. From 1915 until his death, he taught at many institutions, including the Ontario College of Art, the Nova Scotia College of Art, the Montreal Museum of Fine Arts and McGill University. He devoted much of his life to directing art education for children and received wide international recognition for his achievements in the field. After founding children's classes at the Art Gallery of Toronto in 1927, he was invited to South Africa in 1936 and Columbia University in 1938 to initiate courses in the field of art education.

As a teacher and painter, Lismer remained eternally youthful. He possessed an infectious wit and humour which expressed themselves in both words and images. As the Group of Seven's pictorial Boswell, Lismer created a brilliant series of caricatures portraying his colleagues during their meetings and sketching trips. Many of these rapid, visual commentaries round out the outstanding collection of Lismer's works in the McMichael Collection.

Lismer achieved the richest landscape drawings of the Group. These were usually done as ends in themselves and not as studies for paintings. Most of these black and white landscape studies are executed in brush or reed pen and are almost lush in their impact. The best of Lismer's drawings are at the very pinnacle of Canadian graphic art. Marked by a confident bravura, their spirited calligraphy recalls the sweeping shorthand of the finest Oriental masters.

Lismer painted in many parts of Canada. The extent of his travels is well represented in the McMichael Canadian Collection. His fondness for the Maritimes is reflected in works done as far apart in time as *Maritime Village* of 1919 and *Red Anchor*, painted thirty-five years later. The Lake Superior area of Northern Ontario, Quebec and British Columbia are also represented in his sketches and canvases.

Like F.H. Varley, Arthur Lismer attended the Sheffield School of Art in that English city where he was born, and later spent a period at the Antwerp Academy in Belgium. Thus, when he emigrated to Canada in 1911, he was a completely trained artist in an academic tradition. It was the impact of the Canadian landscape, especially that of Northern Ontario, that released Lismer's vigorous sense of design and colour to their utmost. As early as 1914, he was expressing his enthusiasm for the wilderness of Algonquin Park in both paint and words. On his very first trip to the Park, he wrote: "The first night spent in the north and the thrilling days after were turning points in my life". Such letters reveal the eagerness and eloquence he was later to utilize as a spokesman in defence of his own work and that of his fellow members of the Group of Seven.

Although Lismer painted in many parts of Canada, he is best known as the Group of Seven's painter-biographer of the Georgian Bay district. His lush oil sketches of the Bay's vegetation and pine-etched island horizons compose the richest part of his life's work. Summer after summer, he returned to Georgian Bay to search out the lichen-made patterns of its rocks and to track with brush and pen the tangle of its undergrowth. The canvas *Canadian Jungle* in the McMichael Canadian Collection is a key example of Lismer's consuming interest in texture in nature. *Evening Silhouette* is his vision of the Bay islands at their most romantic. The radiant and compelling *Bright Land* captures the essence of Lismer, brilliant, happy, and eternal optimist who justified his joyful faith in life through his long, outgiving career.

ARTHUR LISMER

Rain in the North Country. c. 1920
22.3 x 30.0 cm.
1966.16.112

Dead Tree, Georgian Bay. c. 1926
32.8 x 40.8 cm.
1969.21.1

Canadian Jungle. 1946
44.8 x 53.7 cm.
1966.16.107

ARTHUR LISMER

Pine Wrack. 1939
55.9 x 75.5 cm.
1966.16.111

Stormy Sky, Georgian Bay. 1922
30.3 x 40.4 cm.
L1980.1.40

Lake Superior. 1927
32.3 x 40.1 cm.
1966.16.117

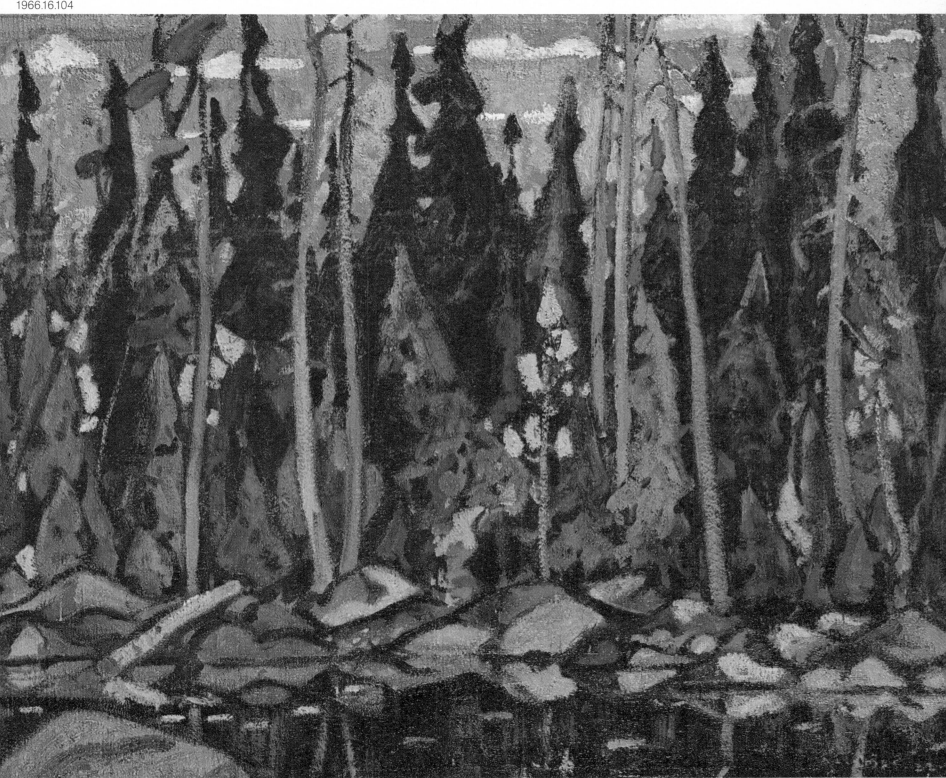

ARTHUR LISMER

In My Studio. 1924
90.8 x 76.2 cm.
1971.10

Gusty Day, Georgian Bay. c. 1920
22.8 x 30.3 cm.
1969.21.2

Evening Silhouette. c. 1926
32.5 x 40.5 cm.
1966.16.108

ARTHUR LISMER

October on the North Shore. 1927
32.3 x 40.8 cm.
1970.14.9

McGregor Bay. 1933
30.0 x 40.6 cm.
1981.27.1

Near Amanda, Georgian Bay. 1947
30.2 x 40.4 cm.
1969.24.3

Negro Head. c. 1940
40.2 x 30.6 cm.
1969.24.2

FREDERICK VARLEY 1881-1969

Varley was the romantic of the Group. His life possessed the same will-of-the-wisp quality that marks many of his poetic landscapes. Until his last years, he was constantly on the move, a questing gypsy of the arts, always, it seems, in search of the perfect landscape, the ideal model.

Varley was tied more closely to European tradition than the other members of the Group. He loved Turner and such other early English landscape painters as Cotnam and Samuel Palmer. His portraits are based in the best tradition of British portrait painting and they have compared with the works of such masters as Augustus John and Ambrose McEvoy.

In his attitude to his subjects, Varley possessed much of the attitude of a mystic. He usually shunned the hard, clear afternoon light favoured so often by his fellow Group painters. He favoured dawn, dusk and twilight and painted more nocturnes than any of his colleagues. Many of his finest canvases, such as *Night Ferry, Vancouver* and *Moonlight at Lynn* are night-pieces. He valued colours for their mystical qualities. Blue, gold, violet and green, he said, were the spiritual hues and these are often dominant in his pictures, even his portraits.

Varley is unquestionably the finest portrayer of people Canada has so far known. He had the imaginative vision, the independence and the technical skills demanded of a great portrait painter. His spirit of independence permitted him to select his sitters and refuse commissions that did not appeal to him. Varley's best portraits of men are penetrating and vigorous, but unquestionably his most memorable studies are those of women. From time to time throughout his life, Varley would have a special model from whom he realized a series of haunting souvenirs in paint. The best of these combine an affectionate tribute to a favoured sitter with consummate craftsmanship.

Varley's greatest strength as a portrait painter was his masterly draughtsmanship. His drawings in pencil, chalk and ink compose an unrivalled Canadian gallery of graphic art. He could draw with a silver-point sensitiveness without sacrificing any of his characteristic vigor. Varley was a singularly masculine painter and even in his most poetic portraits and atmospheric landscapes, he retains the underlying power of a true master of his craft.

Varley emigrated to Toronto from England in 1912. He was introduced to Algonquin Park by Tom Thomson in 1914 and first came to know Georgian Bay through Thomson's patron, Dr. J.M. MacCallum. It was in the Bay area that Varley discovered the material for his early Group landscapes, including his masterpiece, *Stormy Weather, Georgian Bay*. A sketch bearing the same title, painted about the same time, is in the McMichael Canadian Collection. The landscape in this sketch is incorporated in the background of the powerful composition, *Indians Crossing Georgian Bay*, also in the Collection. After Georgian Bay, Varley gave his deepest creative loyalty to the British Columbia landscape. There he found an outlet for his romantic nature in a land of mountains, mists and glaciers that would have enchanted Turner. On the Pacific Coast, between 1926 and 1934, Varley painted the most poetic landscapes in Canadian art. These included the lyrical blue and green *Moonlight at Lynn* of 1933 and the expressionistic canvas *Sphinx Glacier, Mt. Garibaldi*, both in the McMichael Canadian Collection. Varley is also well represented in the Collection as a portrait painter and draughtsman. His examples in this genre include one of his finest feminine studies, *Girl In Red* of 1926, the strongly rendered *Negro Head* of 1940 and the eloquent drawings, *Little Girl* of 1923 and *Indian Girl* of 1927.

Dead Tree, Garibaldi Park. c. 1928
20.3 x 38.1 cm.
1966.16.142

Mountain Portage. 1925
50.5 x 61.0 cm.
1966.16.141

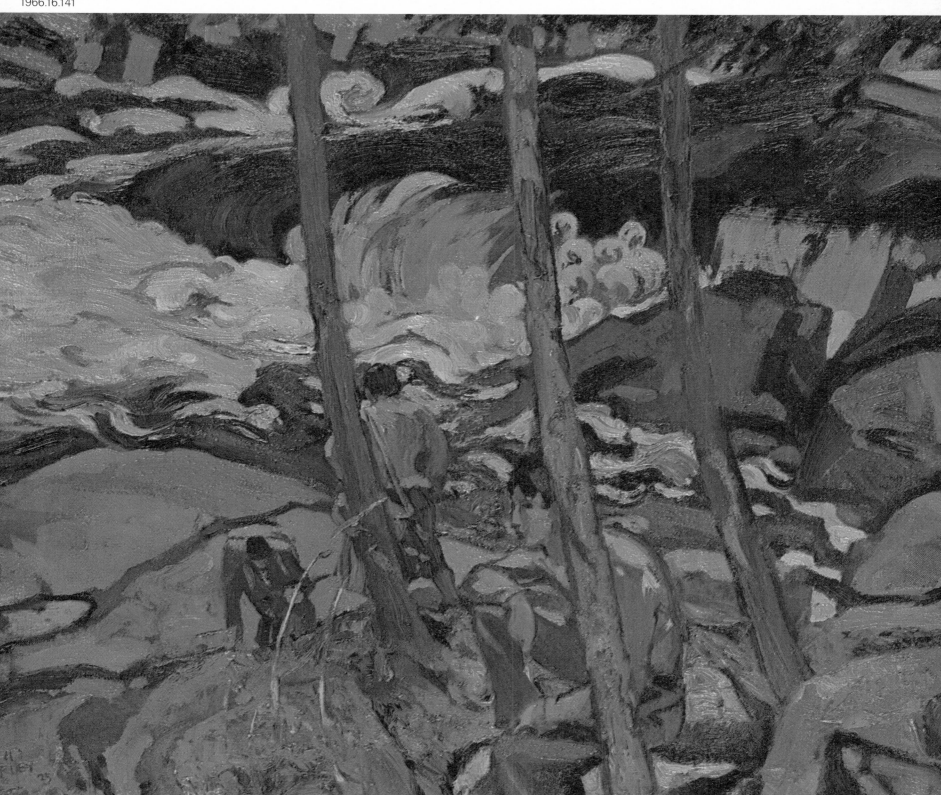

F. H. VARLEY

Portrait of a Man. c. 1950
69.3 x 45.5 cm.
1966.16.138

Little Girl. c. 1923
36.7 x 28.7 cm.
1969.9.1

Stormy Weather, Georgian Bay. c. 1920
20.7 x 26.6 cm.
1966.16.139

F. H. VARLEY

FRANKLIN CARMICHAEL

A Northern Silver Mine. 1930
101.5 x 121.2 cm.
1971.9

FRANKLIN CARMICHAEL 1890-1945

Many of Franklin Carmichael's finest sketches and canvases were painted near his hometown of Orillia during the early 1920s. During those early Group of Seven years, Carmichael was working fulltime as a commercial designer, and was obliged to find his subject matter on journeys relatively close to Toronto. Despite this, his Orillia paintings lack none of the richness or grandeur of his colleagues' compositions created in the wilderness much further north. Carmichael's early Group-period works reveal a rich paint impasto and glowing colour, suggesting an almost buoyant enthusiasm. He delighted in the rich fabric of autumn foliage and excelled in its depiction. Such sketches as *Autumn Tapestry, Autumn Woods, Scarlet Hilltop* and *Autumn Orillia* in the McMichael Canadian Collection show the artist's love of natural pattern at its best.

Like his younger colleague, A.J. Casson, Carmichael had a fondness for portraying the characteristic stores, barns and houses of rural Ontario settlements. During the 1930s, throughout the southern part of the province and along the shore of Lake Superior, he found isolated dwellings or small villages from which he composed many watercolours, drawings and a few oils.

His renderings of farmhouses, barns and old homesteads in Whitefish Village, Severn Bridge and many other Ontario communities suggest the same lived-in intimacy as A.Y. Jackson's portrayals of such Quebec villages as St. Tite des Caps, St. Urbain and St. Pierre.

Franklin Carmichael's large canvases are relative rarities. Although he was dedicated to painting landscape, economic necessity led him to spend much of his lifetime at commercial art and teaching. Unable to concentrate for long periods on major works, he turned to the medium of watercolour for many of his best achievements. His large watercolours possess a crystalline clarity of colour and authority of design in their transparent washes. Carmichael's dedication to watercolour made him a co-founder of the Canadian Society of Painters in Water Colour.

Carmichael's first visit to Lake Superior in 1925 opened up new worlds of form and space to him. The vast panoramas of hills and lakes unrolling before his vision as far as the eye could see captured his imagination. His landscape compositions expanded to include large stretches of sky and simplified silhouettes of whale-back rises, the very opposite to his earlier close-up bushland paintings. His colour changed also, from thick golds, vermilion, and emerald greens to smoother, dark ultramarines, greys, ochres, siennas and blacks. The emphasis in these compositions became mainly horizontal — a tendency that continued throughout the balance of his career, persisting into the superb impressions of the LaCloche hills painted during the thirties. Carmichael's fondness for panoramic compositions can be studied in the McMichael Canadian Collection through such typical canvases as *Northern Tundra* of 1931, *Grace Lake* of 1933, and such later sketches as *LaCloche Panorama* and *La Cloche Silhouette*, both painted in 1939.

Carmichael was a superb designer and graphic artist. With Edwin Holgate, Carmichael was the only Group of Seven member to devote much attention to the art of wood-engraving. His disciplined dedication to the craft resulted in many sparkling prints, including the pristine small illustrations for the book, *Thorn Apple Tree*, published in 1942. These tiny engravings, which measure less than three by four inches, are replete with vigorously rendered detail and are masterpieces of their kind. They rank Carmichael among the few distinguished book illustrators produced in Canada. Another, very different example of Carmichael's remarkable sense of design can be seen in his crisp tempera translation of landscape, *Waterfall*, 1943 in the McMichael Canadian Collection.

Scarlet Hilltop. 1922
24.6 x 30.2 cm.
1966.16.10

Bolton Hills. c. 1922
24.6 x 30.2 cm.
1966.16.2

Mirror Lake. 1929
44.0 x 54.5 cm.
1976.8

FRANKLIN CARMICHAEL

October Gold. 1922
120.0 x 98.7 cm.
1966.16.1

La Cloche Panorama. 1939
25.4 x 30.5 cm.
1966.16.8

La Cloche Silhouette. 1939
25.5 x 30.5 cm.
1966.16.7

A.J. CASSON 1898-

For the most part, A.J. Casson left the more elemental and epic landscape of the northland to other members of the Group of Seven. His serene pictorial compositions have emerged mainly from southern and central Ontario settings. Particularly, he has been the pictorial biographer of the small communities of Ontario. He has celebrated such towns and villages as Bancroft, Glen Williams, Kleinburg, Parry Sound, Norval and Salem. His crisp, deliberate style has been ideally suited to depict the tidy rustic architecture, with its neat verandahs, almost puritan air of no-nonsense form, dressed up with an occasional flight of fancy in the guise of gingerbread "fretwork". Although human figures usually play only bit parts in Casson's canvases, his village paintings are nevertheless redolent of humanity. His houses, barns and churches usually have the air of being lived in. This impression is only fortified when he introduces inhabitants hanging out washing, hauling water or bending before a March blizzard.

Casson was basically a conservative within the Group of Seven. He inherited from his older colleague, Franklin Carmichael, a high regard for craftsmanship. There are no accidents or meaningless flourishes in his creative vocabulaire. Although his small on-the-spot oil panels are executed with a fresh and direct vigour, his larger canvases based on them are composed slowly and with great care. As a result, Casson's stylistic evolution has been a gradual one, moving with a seeming inevitability, and without any sudden leaps into new techniques or thematic novelties.

Casson's independence and respect for tradition brought him the respect of a wide spectrum of artists and allowed him to be a President of the Royal Canadian Academy as well as a member of the pathfinding Group of Seven and the Canadian Group of Painters.

For many years, Casson joined his career as a painter with that of a designer and executive for Sampson Matthews Limited, a Toronto printing house, where Carmichael and other distinguished Canadian painters were employed. There, Casson produced some of the most outstanding commercial art ever produced in Canada.

Casson is one of the finest watercolourists in Canadian art. He learned his technique from Carmichael and, with him, was a founding member of the Canadian Society of Painters in Water Colour. It is in his watercolours that Casson's design sense can be seen at its purest. Crisp, almost dry, in their rendering, their washes are placed with precision within a careful framework of drawing. Some of Casson's best-known large paintings, such as *The White Pine* in the McMichael Canadian Collection, existed originally as watercolours.

Casson is represented in the McMichael Canadian Collection by over half-a-century of his art. The earliest examples are a number of nude studies in pencil and wash executed in 1917. The landscapes on view begin with a number of superb sketches from the early 1920s — *Trees* 1920, *Rock And Sky* 1921, *Haliburton Woods* 1924 and *Poplars* 1925. Casson's most personal vision is first revealed in the *Sombreland, Lake Superior* and *Pike Lake* sketches of 1929 and the early village studies, *Norval* and *Kleinburg* of 1929. Casson had by then found his own manner and themes and from then on, through to his LaCloche, Bancroft and Quebec paintings, his evolution was a continuing enrichment of familiar themes.

Kleinburg. c. 1929
23.9 x 28.5 cm.
1966.16.124

Casson Lake. c. 1976
30.5 x 38.1 cm.
1981.13

Pike Lake. c. 1929
43.0 x 51.5 cm.
1968.7.6

Summer Hillside. 1945
50.7 x 61.1 cm.
1972.9

Drowned Land, Algoma. c. 1918
45.9 x 54.8 cm.
1966.15.1

FRANK JOHNSTON

1888-1949

Frank Johnston's 1918 paintings of Algoma are as compelling as anything done by the Group of Seven at that time. Although he remained with the Group only briefly, Johnston's short contribution to it was a very eloquent one. The best of his sketches of the period are consummately designed, richly painted tangles of branches, evergreens and foliage. From the beginning of his career, Johnston had a highly developed dramatic sense in his approach to nature. In his tempera paintings done shortly after World War I, he captured the immensity of the northern solitudes in compositions bearing such titles as *The Guardian of the Gorge*. Pictorial drama is present, too, in such large northern canvases as *Fire Swept Algoma* of 1920. Like so many of his colleagues, Johnston for many years made his main living as a teacher. After leaving the Group, he turned to teaching for twenty years, first as Principal of the Winnipeg School of Art and then as a teacher at the Ontario College of Art and later as Director of his own art school on the shores of Georgian Bay. In the latter part of his career, Johnston devoted himself to a technique of almost photographic realism with which he recorded life in Southern Ontario farm and bushland, and life in the Canadian Arctic. These later paintings are executed in a medium which allowed the artist to capture the glitter of sunlight and the smallest details of texture. His obvious technical brilliance made Johnston one of the most popular and financially successful artists of his time.

Moose Pond. 1918
26.4 x 33.8 cm.
1972.18.14

LEMOINE FITZGERALD 1890-1956

LeMoine FitzGerald was the only western Canadian painter to become a member of the Group of Seven. FitzGerald's membership came at the very end of the Group's existence, too late to have any but an honorary significance. He was, in fact, too removed physically, in Winnipeg, and too different in his approach to landscape painting to have fitted in with the Group in their heyday.

FitzGerald was exceedingly individualistic, both as a personality and artist. Although he was involved in teaching at the Winnipeg School of Art for a quarter of a century, he was very much of a loner as a creative painter. His serene, pointillist canvases were achieved mostly during his holidays, using an immensely painstaking technique. It is not surprising that FitzGerald's paintings are few in number when one realizes how slowly his style obliged him to work and how little free creative time was at his disposal.

The paintings FitzGerald achieved earned him a major place in Canadian art. He might fairly be described as the Seurat or Vermeer of our country's painting. He usually chose the simplest, most commonplace of themes — a garage, a backyard, a few apples, a milk pitcher or a plant in a window — and by the sheer intensity of his vision and refinement of craftsmanship converted these into works of art that, once seen, impress themselves upon the memory. FitzGerald studied for a short period at New York's Art Students League and, as a realist, shared the special magic to intensify ordinary visual experience that marks such great Americans as Charles Sheeler and Georgia O'Keefe.

Because of the limited creative time at his disposal, FitzGerald spent much of it executing drawings in pencil and pen and ink. These are as considered and complete as any of his paintings, and take an outstanding place in Canadian graphic art. They are drawings complete as an end in themselves and not preparatory notes for later development into canvases. In his last years, FitzGerald did a number of pure abstractions which reveal the same stylistic and technical concentration which typify his earlier still-lifes and landscapes. These abstractions represented a logical extension of the artist's lifetime pursuit of form.

The Little Plant. 1947
60.5 x 45.7 cm.
1969.2.4

LIONEL LEMOINE FITZGERALD

Oak Bluff. 1950
27.2 x 37.9 cm.
1981.41.9

The Embrace. c. 1925
26.8 x 32.7 cm.
1969.2.5

Tree Trunk. 1939
28.3 x 37.1 cm. (sight)
1981.41.5

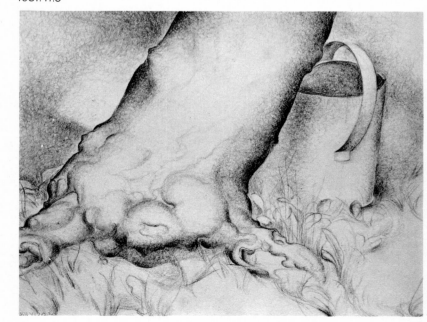

The Harvester. c. 1921
66.8 x 59.5 cm.
1981.41.3

LIONEL LEMOINE FITZGERALD

DAVID B. MILNE

Painting Place: Brown and Black. c. 1926
30.7 x 41.0 cm.
1981.41.1

114

DAVID MILNE 1882-1953

David Milne was the quiet man of his generation of Canadian artists. Eloquent in paint, a descriptive writer in his occasional prose, Milne talked little about his art. Unlike the sociable Group of Seven members, Milne only rarely came into contact with his fellow painters. A loner — virtually a recluse — for most of his life, he was the opposite of a self-propagandist. Like Tom Thomson, he allowed his work to speak for him, and it did, in an original, intense and unforgettable way.

As an artist, David Milne made great demands upon his talent. He was a perfectionist who could paint a dozen variations of the same theme until he was finally satisfied that he had refined his statement down to its essentials. As a result of this approach to art, Milne's compositions may appear deceptively simple at first glance. The depth of experience, judgment and technical skill required to compress such pictorial poetry into a few lines and colours can only be appreciated through acquaintance with his art. Economy of style in Milne's case is the result of an almost monastic dedication. Milne's art is the closest to the great Oriental painters in its eloquent simplicity and pure visual poetry.

The refinement of Milne's style grew through a progression of styles over a period of more than forty years. His canvases before the First World War were heavily pigmented, and boldly drawn in pure vermilions, olive greens, blues, ochres and black.

These brought him international notice in the famous Armory Show at New York in 1913. Milne was one of the many leading Canadian painters who studied at New York's Art Students League and much of his career was spent in the northern part of New York State until 1928. His lean, luminous dry brush watercolours and oils done in the Catskills, the lower Berkshires and the Adirondacks remain among his most commanding achievements. Upon his return to Canada, Milne painted for varying periods, at Temagami, Palgrave, Six Mile Lake and in Toronto. His colour drypoint etchings of Toronto buildings take a special place in his graphic work.

The McMichael Canadian Collection includes significant examples of Milne's achievement from early canvases of the 1914 period to the almost calligraphic watercolours of his last years.

Milne's early New York oils are the most richly coloured and robust of all his works. They are painted with a loaded brush and are almost encrusted in texture. The importance of these early canvases is underlined by the fact that several of them were included in the great, revolutionary Armory Show of 1913 in Manhattan. In that historic exhibition, Milne's work was displayed on the same walls as Picasso, Cézanne, Kandinsky, Matisse and Gauguin. His work can be compared with that of the American master, Maurice Prendergast. In the McMichael Canadian Collection, the early phase of Milne may be seen in the oils *bright leaves and dark woods* c. 1910-11, *Black* 1914, *Lilies* c. 1913-14 and the watercolour *Relaxation* of 1916. In the years following, Milne's style became increasingly leaner in technique and more restricted in colour.

The canvases and watercolours of Boston Corners, Lake Placid and the Adirondacks painted between 1920 and 1928 are lean in execution to the point of a drybrush technique. They are almost Oriental in their subtlety of drawing and restricted hues. In the McMichael Canadian Collection, this phase of Milne's art is richly revealed in such oils as *houses in sunlight* c. 1910-11, *The Gully* 1920, *Blue Church* 1920, *Haystack* 1923, *valley at Lake Placid III* 1925 and the two small canvases of Clarke's house of c. 1923.

Side Door, Clarke's House. c. 1923
30.5 x 40.6 cm.
1976.25.2

Back of Clarke's House. 1923
30.8 x 40.8 cm.
1966.16.27

Haystack. 1923
41.2 x 51.2 cm.
1966.16.26

houses in sunlight. c. 1910-11
44.5 x 51.5 cm.
1966.16.19

Blue Church. 1920
46.0 x 56.2 cm.
1966.16.22

Black. 1914
50.7 x 61.0 cm.
1966.16.23

Station, Elevator and Cloud. 1932
30.9 x 41.0 cm.
1969.26.3

DAVID B. MILNE

Pansies No. 1. 1941
38.1 x 55.3 cm.
1969.2.1

Boat Houses, Glenmore Hotel. 1926
40.8 x 51.0 cm.
1966.16.20

Red Plate. 1939
35.4 x 48.8 cm.
1969.5.2

DAVID B. MILNE

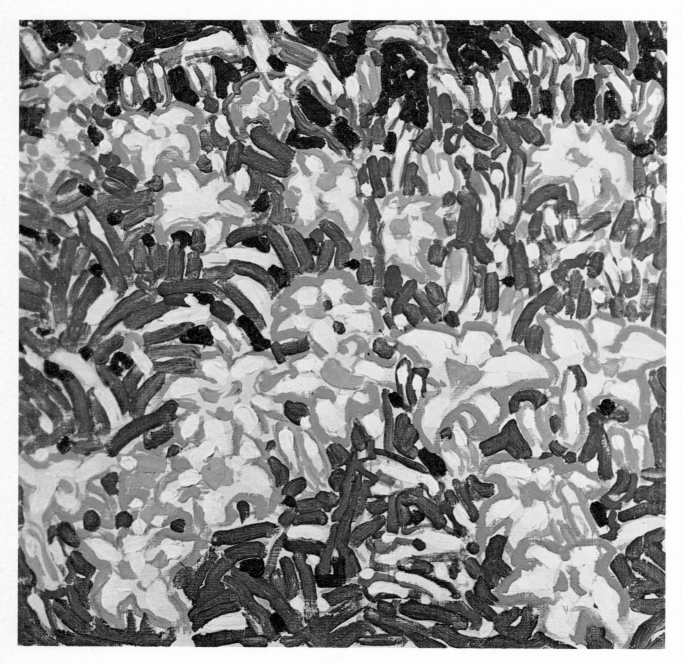

Lilies. c. 1913-14
51.0 x 51.0 cm.
1966.16.18

Fishermen's Houses. c. 1933
51.0 x 61.2 cm.
1977.36

EDWIN HOLGATE

Mother and Daughter. 1926
61.0 x 60.0 cm.
1971.16

EDWIN HOLGATE

1892-1977

    Edwin Holgate became a late addition to the Group of Seven in 1931. By then, he had already established a firm reputation for his figure paintings and West Coast and Laurentian landscapes. A student in Montreal under the same William Brymner who had taught A.Y. Jackson, Clarence Gagnon and many other important painters, Holgate early showed a preference for painting humanity, an inclination shared in the Group of Seven only by F.H. Varley. Holgate spent a number of years in Paris painting the figure before returning to Canada in the early 1920s to begin the series of nudes in northern landscapes for which he is best known. Apart from a trip to the Skeena River area of British Columbia with A.Y. Jackson in 1926, Holgate remained a Quebec-based painter. His landscapes were mostly painted in the Laurentians, where he lived much of his life. These are carefully patterned, ruggedly executed compositions, but rarely achieve the creative involvement found in his best figure and portrait studies.

    Holgate's robust portraits form an eloquent gallery of Canadians, including lumberjacks, *habitants,* pilots, and such familiar creative figures as humorist Stephen Leacock. At their finest, there is a masculine monumentality to Holgate's portrayals. He always used a direct, no-nonsense manner of painting which has its origins in the Cézanne-oriented painters of the first two decades of the century. The same vigorous approach marks his large portrait drawings in charcoal.

    During periods of his career, Holgate shared the same financial difficulties that beset some other members of the Group of Seven. They solved their economic difficulties by

Melting Snow. 1948
21.6 x 27.0 cm.
1966.11

teaching, but Holgate turned to wall decoration. He did many murals of varying distinction, the best known being his effective designs for the Totem Pole Room at Ottawa's Chateau Laurier Hotel which regrettably no longer exist except in photographs.

It was only after the Group-of-Seven years that Holgate finally undertook to teach at the Art Association of Montreal from 1935 to 1940. Many of Canada's most gifted contemporary painters, including Jean-Paul Lemieux and Stanley Cosgrove, benefited from his instruction. Among the talents Holgate brought to his teaching post were his skills as a book illustrator and wood engraver. His wood engravings of nudes and French Canadian interiors include some of the finest of all original Canadian prints. Holgate shared a passionate concern for rural Quebec with such artists as Clarence Gagnon and Horatio Walker. In his own dramatically designed black and white compositions, he made permanent that passing phase of history.

The Cellist. 1923
128.0 x 97.5 cm.
1972.18.2

Nude. c. 1922
32.7 x 26.1 cm.
1968.10

CLARENCE GAGNON 1881-1942

Clarence Gagnon was the pictorial bard of rural Quebec. The life and land of the *habitant* inspired him to some of the most engaging paintings ever made of the Canadian scene. His consummately drawn, high-keyed canvases are vibrant with the atmosphere and activity of French Canada.

Gagnon studied under William Brymner in Montreal and did his earliest records of Quebec at the turn of the century. After five years of study in Paris he returned to Canada in 1919 to begin his pictorial salutes to the colourful settlements of the St. Lawrence and the Laurentians. Although he spent most of his later years in France and Norway, his affections and art remained steeped in the life of his native land.

It was while living in Europe that Gagnon created what must be considered his most ambitious and remarkable creative achievement — the illustrations for the Quebec masterpiece *Maria Chapdelaine* by Louis Hémon. In the fifty-four paintings done to ornament this volume published in Paris in 1934, Gagnon equalled the eloquence of Hémon's symbolic tribute to French Canada with miniature masterpieces of his own.

Nowhere in Canadian annals has illustration reached to such heights as art. And no other Canadian artist possessed the combination of special talents to equal Gagnon's graphic eloquence. The illustrations for *Maria Chapdelaine* combine all of the factual specifics demanded of literary illustration along with tonal poetry and power of design as paintings in their own right. Sometimes as small as 17 by 20 centimetres, these amazing little paintings take a special place in the art of their time. They are, in turn, stark, tragic, gay, brave and tender. They move the emotions as much as they command admiration as art. Their subject matter is as timeless as their expression. From first communion to last rites, here are the vanishing traditions of rural Quebec in their totality.

For the first time, the Maria Chapdelaine illustrations can now be seen and enjoyed at will by the public.

During his lifetime, they were the most treasured possessions of the late Colonel R.S. McLaughlin, who reserved a special room for their display. It was always his wish that the paintings should never be separated. By giving them to the McMichael Canadian Collection, he was assured that they would remain together in perpetuity.

Clarence Gagnon first visited his favourite St. Lawrence painting site, Baie Saint-Paul at the turn of the century, in 1900. There, he discovered his favourite themes of pastel-hued village streets, wayside shrines and parish churches. The quiet, rustic life of that early period finds its reflection in Gagnon's brush through the *habitant* figures at work, baking bread at open ovens, riding ox-pulled sleds or weaving on the doorsteps of their cottages. For the rest of his life, whether living in Quebec or Europe, Gagnon sustained his interest in the rural life of the lower St. Lawrence and Laurentians. Just before his death, he devoted his days toward a project to build a French-Canadian village museum to perpetuate the image of early *habitant* life.

Gagnon's great gifts as a painter have frequently overshadowed his abilities as a graphic artist. His series of etchings achieved during the first decade of this century are probably the finest ever done in this country. He also realized many distinguished figure drawings in the media of pencil and pastel.

Gagnon always carried his native Quebec within him wherever he travelled. Some of his best Canadian landscapes were painted in his Paris studio from sketches made at home. When he visited Norway or Switzerland, it was usually to sketch the snow which formed so much a part of his studies of scenes from his native land.

October, a thousand shades of orange and yellow. 1928-33
17.7 x 20.0 cm.
1969.4.29

MARIA CHAPDELAINE

Maria Chapdelaine by the French author and journalist, Louis Hémon, is the classic novel of French Canadian *habitant* life. First published in 1914, the year after Hémon's death, it is unquestionably the most illustrated of all books about Canada. More than a dozen artists have decorated various editions including such distinguished Canadians as Suzor-Côté and Thoreau MacDonald.

The most famous edition of *Maria Chapdelaine* is that illustrated by Clarence Gagnon and published in 1934 by the Paris publishing house of Mornay. This volume is now one of the most sought-after of all books relating to Canada. It was first issued in a numbered deluxe edition of 2,000 copies, of which the McMichael Canadian Collection displays number 1545.

The 54 original illustrations for *Maria Chapdelaine* were presented by the late R.S. McLaughlin to the McMichael Canadian Collection and now form one of its most treasured exhibits.

...a paradise must it be this country to the South.
...quels paradis ce devaient être ces contrées du sud.
20.7 x 20.3 cm.
1969.4.42

...some peculiar quality of sweetness and peace in that house in the woods.
...ces gestes ...revêtaient de douceur cette maison isolée dans les bois.
22.1 x 23.4 cm.
1969.4.9

...we have only dogs to draw our sleds, fine strong dogs ...
...on n'a que des chiens pour atteler aux traineaux, de beaux chiens forts ...
17.8 x 21.6 cm.
1969.4.12

...and chest against the bar, threw all their weight upon it ...
...et pesaient de toute leur force, la poitrine appuyé sur la barre de bois ...
20.4 x 20.7 cm.
1969.4.18

...the moment for laying wood is also that of the slaughtering.
...l'époque où l'on empile le bois est aussi celle où l'on "fait boucherie".
19.0 x 19.3 cm.
1969.4.30

...were she to marry a man like Eutrope and accept a life of rude toil...
...ce qui l'attendait si elle l'épousait... une vie de labeur grossier...
19.9 x 19.5 cm.
1969.4.44

...mosquitoes rose in swarms from the cut hay, tormenting the workers...
...les mouches et les maringouins les harcelaient de leurs piqûres.
19.0 x 20.4 cm.
1969.4.24

...from dawn until nightfall, spending all strength in heavy tasks...
...du matin au soir, elle faisait le ménage et l'ordinaire...
21.9 x 22.0 cm.
1969.4.51

CLARENCE A. GAGNON

...while the priest performed the sacred rites...
...pendant que le prêtre accomplissait les gestes consacrés...
19.5 x 20.3 cm.
1969.4.49

...the two men took the double-handed saw, and sawed, and sawed.
...les deux hommes prirent le "godendard" et scièrent, scièrent, scièrent...
18.8 x 22.0 cm.
1969.4.31

...at every fall where logs jam and pile, would be found the river-drivers.
...à toutes les chutes, il faut encore le concours des draveurs forts.
20.5 x 21.0 cm.
1969.4.20

...I will marry you as you asked me to...in the Spring after this Spring...
...je vous marierai, le printemps d'après ce printemps-ci...
21.0 x 22.0 cm.
1969.4.54

EMILY CARR 1871-1945

Few artists have wedded nature and the human spirit so passionately as Emily Carr. A headlong, single-minded mingling of art with her love for her native British Columbia produced the finest expressionist painting Canada has known.

Emily Carr's long career was plagued by difficulties, financial and otherwise. Her creative demands upon herself, a lack of public appreciation and the pressures of poverty pursued her throughout her lifetime. She was forced to run a boarding house and make souvenir pottery to survive. For years, she was without the sustenance to paint. Despite this, with the encouragement of a few friends such as Lawren Harris, she persisted to create many masterpieces which include some of the most loved canvases in the history of Canadian art.

Emily Carr's first important works were closely related to the life and lore of the West Coast Indians. She spent much time among them, and from their totems, graveyards and churches composed some of her most dramatic paintings. Her canvases of the early 1912 series record such Indian villages as Skidigate, Tanov, Gitwangak and Alert Bay. In them, survive the houses, poles and people of an era then vanishing, as the career of Emily Carr was to cease for a period shortly afterwards. When she began painting again in the 1920s, Emily Carr was to approach the Indian material in a different mood and style.

By now, she was more concerned in capturing the spirit of the Indian structures than in recording them log by log. She simplified the totem poles and house poles, with their surrounding landscape, into abstracted designs which echoed the rich, carved rhythms of the Indian art itself.

By the 1930s, Emily Carr's attention turned almost completely to the B.C. coastal shorelines and forests. Her design-sense learned from the Indians and Cézanne found a looser expression. Her skies, earth and foliage became joined into a single swirling whole, reflecting her subjective feeling about her themes rather than their material facts.

Emily Carr's career as an artist spanned almost a half a century. Her earliest works are reticent watercolours done following studies in San Francisco and London. Her true power of expression first emerges in a series of brilliantly coloured canvases in the *fauve* manner painted in Brittany, France from 1910 to 1912. Upon her return to Canada in 1912, Emily Carr adapted the rich *fauve* style to portrayals of West Coast Indian villages and landscapes. Two examples of her work in this manner in the McMichael Canadian Collection are *Brittany, France* 1911 and *House And Garden*, probably painted in 1912.

By the early 1930s, Emily Carr had already achieved such familiar masterpieces as *Indian Church*, exhibited in 1933 by the Canadian Group of Painters. Her compelling and mystical wood interiors were also attracting the attention of a few discriminating collectors. The National Gallery of Canada had already purchased her west coast studies as early as 1928 and continued to do so through the 1930s and after. In the McMichael Collection the magnificent landscapes of the 1930s are represented by such superb, rhythmic compositions as *Reforestation* 1936, *Shoreline* 1936, *Old Tree At Dusk* c. 1936 and *Edge Of The Forest* c. 1935.

Although she lived mostly alone, Emily Carr created a pictorial universe for others. From a caravan, in which she travelled up and down the British Columbia coast, she created an ageless art of the spirit to be shared by future Canadians for countless generations.

Emily Carr was a gifted writer and much of her life story and philosophy is to be found in such remarkable autobiographical books as *Klee Wyck, Growing Pains, House Of All Sorts* and *Hundreds And Thousands*.

Edge of the Forest. c. 1935
86.7 x 58.4 cm.
1969.20

A Haida Village. c. 1929
82.7 x 60.7 cm.
1974.18.1

Brittany, France. c. 1911
46.8 x 61.7 cm.
1974.11.3

Swaying. c. 1936
35.5 x 45.5 cm.
1966.5.2

Old Tree at Dusk. c. 1936
112.0 x 68.5 cm.
1968.7.13

Corner of Kitwancool Village. c. 1930
111.1 x 68.6 cm.
1977.42

EMILY CARR

Shoreline. 1936
68.0 x 111.5 cm.
1966.2.1

New Growth. c. 1936
46.4 x 65.1 cm.
1972.10

134

Reforestation. 1936
110.0 x 67.2 cm.
1966. 16.17

Haytime, Knowlton Quebec. c. 1930
56.7 x 67.0 cm.
1972.12

ALBERT ROBINSON

1881-1956

The career of Albert H. Robinson was beset and shortened by illness. Rheumatism crippled him during the last decades of his life and his painting career was limited to a span of little more than twenty years. In that time, he produced some of the most subtle colour compositions ever painted of the Canadian landscape. The very earliest of these were of subjects in Europe, where he painted with his close friend A.Y. Jackson in Brittany in 1911. The delicate hues he favoured then were transferred permanently to the Quebec scene in the group of sketches and canvases he painted during the 1920s. These views of such areas as the Laurentians, Baie Saint-Paul, Saint-Fidele and Murray Bay are among the best loved and most sought-after views of French Canada.

Loosely rendered, in an almost patch-work technique of square edged, lozenge-shaped strokes, they represent a gentle and poetic response to the Canadian landscape. Robinson was primarily a painter of winter, but there appears no bitterness, starkness or challenge in his snow-clad hills and villages. His was a pastel vision. It is as though his pink, grey and blue dipped brush removed the severity from the land and left behind only the silver sunlight and the sound of sleigh bells. Like the happy French master, Raoul Dufy, Robinson turned almost everything he painted into a land a little gayer than the reality we see. Robinson's gentle tonal art is represented in the McMichael Canadian Collection by four canvases, including *St. Joseph* with its sapphire-like patches of water and several sketches of the villages he was so fond of recording.

Afternoon, Sainte Simeon. c. 1924
56.0 x 66.5 cm.
1977.35

J. W. MORRICE

J.W. MORRICE 1865-1924

J.W. Morrice was one of the gypsies of Canadian art. Born in Montreal, his wanderlust career took him among other places to Paris, Venice, Brittany, Spain, North Africa, Tunis, England, Cuba and Trinidad. Originally intended for a career at law, he first began to paint in the Toronto area while studying at the University of Toronto. Immediately upon finishing his legal studies, he headed for Paris to study art. For most of his life after that Paris remained his creative headquarters.

Morrice was a close friend of Canadian fellow-painters Maurice Cullen and William Brymner. Together, the trio had an immeasurable impact upon the country's art. Brymner taught A.Y. Jackson, Edwin Holgate, Clarence Gagnon, Helen McNicoll and many other important national painters. Both Morrice and Cullen were major influences upon such significant figures as A.Y. Jackson, Goodridge Roberts, Jacques de Tonnancour, John Lyman and Robert Pilot. Jackson often described Morrice and Cullen as the two who formed "the backbone" of his career.

Although he was an expatriate for most of his life, Morrice is one of the most popular and sought-after Canadian painters and is regarded by many, especially in Quebec, as our greatest painter. Certainly, Morrice has received the widest international recognition of any of our past artists. He was a close friend of the great French masters Henri Matisse and Albert Marquet, and the important British painter Matthew Smith, and shared painting trips with all of them. Morrice's last late canvases, painted in the West Indies under the colour influence of Matisse are certainly among the best ever realized by a Canadian-born artist. Today, European critics agree that Morrice played a very real, if relatively minor role in the history of French art during the post-impressionist period.

Probably the most personal aspect of Morrice's art was his abbreviated drawing style. This loose, economic manner was already established as early as 1909 when he painted the famous *The Ferry, Quebec* and continues through to the last glowing Trinidad canvases.

Some of Morrice's most telling creations are the small pochades or quick sketches in oil he made in panels while sitting in city cafes or at the seashore. The seventeen examples of this type in the McMichael Canadian Collection reveal the artist's changing styles over a period of more than twenty years.

These range from an early grey, heavily painted panel *Notre Dame* to a luminous, simplified, sunlit view of *Tunis*, painted toward the end of his career. Although most of these works measure a mere twelve by fifteen centimetres, each of them is a complete composition. The intimacy and warmth of these spontaneous notations puts them into a place of their own in Canadian art. The technique used to create these small oils was a combination of rubbed-in glazes and brushwork accents. Morrice carried a little sketchbox in his coat pocket and would stop to quickly record any on-the-spot scenes which appealed to him, whether they were in a country field or along a busy boulevard.

Although Morrice was restless in his travels, his painting arose from an inner creative constant. He turned natural forms to his own creative ends, regardless of whether he was in France, Quebec, North Africa, Cuba or Trinidad. His style of painting is unmistakable, regardless of theme.

Despite the influence upon him of several great artist-friends, Morrice remained his own creative man. There is a contagious charm about his art in general which is little short of pictorial magic. Morrice was a compulsive painter who recorded life from a deep love of the world around him.

Tunis. c. 1920
23.5 x 32.5 cm.
1968.25.22

Sailboat. c. 1911
12.4 x 15.3 cm.
1969.5.1

Algiers. c. 1919
25.0 x 23.5 cm.
1968.22.1

Landscape in Trinidad. c. 1921
38.0 x 46.6 cm.
1975.31

The Jetty. c. 1918
12.4 x 15.3 cm.
1968.7.21

Along the Bank. c. 1909
12.3 x 15.2 cm.
1968.7.30

Paris. c. 1909
12.3 x 15.3 cm.
1968.7.28

Village Square. c. 1918
12.1 x 15.3 cm
1968.7.20

Indian Girl. c. 1932
76.3 x 61.0 cm.
1966.16.13

Cobalt. c. 1928
25.5 x 33.8 cm.
1966.16.16

YVONNE McKAGUE HOUSSER 1898-

Although Yvonne Housser was not a member of the Group of Seven she was closely associated with the movement and was a founding member of the Canadian Group of Painters which succeeded the original Group in 1933. In canvases painted in the late twenties and early thirties, she concentrated on portraying Northern Ontario mining towns. These studies vividly capture the special character of those isolated settlements, whose frame houses scattered on a sea of rock were among the most telling symbols of a desperate era in Canadian economic history.

The career of Yvonne Housser represents the restless, questing spirit of many artists born at the turn of this century. From a near-impressionist European style of the early twenties, she moved through a Group-oriented landscape period, a finely realized series of Indian portraits and Mexican scenes to the almost pure abstractions of the 1960s. Despite these changes from style to style, her evolution was a logical and organic one, and at no time do we find a change in direction for the mere sake of fashion.

Yvonne Housser taught at the Ontario College of Art for some thirty years and, like the creative teacher she was, continued her own studies under such international masters as Hans Hofmann at Cape Cod and Emil Bistram in Mexico. Her substantial body of paintings done over many decades represents only a part of her restless dedication to the creative life of Canada as artist, teacher and counsellor to many of her colleagues.

Autumn Forest c. 1935
61.0 x 76.0 cm.
1969.25.3

Slumber. c. 1935
81.0 x 101.0 cm.
1969.25.4

Benedicta. c. 1935
183.0 x 121.0 cm.
1969.25.6

RANDOLPH HEWTON 1888-1960

Randolph Hewton was one of the best trained of all Canadian painters. Beginning as a student under Montreal's famed William Brymner in 1903, he later studied and painted in Paris from 1908-1913. In Paris, Hewton shared his studio for a time with A.Y. Jackson, and the two painted together in rural France. Their joint exhibition of these European works held at the Art Association of Montreal in 1913 first brought Hewton and Jackson to public attention. Hewton later exhibited with the Group of Seven as an invited contributor. His art career was cut short when he decided to enter the business world in the early 1920s. Although he continued to paint some fine canvases — particularly of figure and portrait subjects — one can only guess what Hewton might have achieved if he had continued to concentrate upon his art.

143

Artist Unknown
Standing Figure.
27.5 x 20.0 x 4.0 cm.
1975.69.4

Pauta
Bear (rampant).
59.5 x 29.0 x 16.0 cm.
1975.69.5

INUIT ART

One recent summer I had the great good fortune to visit Cape Dorset on Baffin Island, and sit with Pitseolak, many of whose fine prints are represented in The McMichael Canadian Collection, and talk with her about life.

She told me that she knew hers had been an unusual life. She was born in a skin tent, yet lived to hear on the radio that two men had landed on the moon. Like other Inuit artists, with great veracity, she puts her life into her drawings. "I draw the old ways", she says, "the things we did long ago, and I draw the things I have never seen — the spirits and monsters". One day as we talked, she pointed to a print of hers of a tent in a book, and said to our young interpreter who, in blue jeans and modern gear, seemed to come from a very different world. "A long time ago, we used to live like that in the seal-skin tents — you wouldn't believe it, but it's really true!"

Inuit artists detail for us, in a manner that surely seems "really true", home life in the tents and igloos, aspects of the hunt, childbirth, death, and the spectrum of Inuit life. They record beliefs and legends, stories of true events, and, of course, they give us a marvellous diversity of animals and birds.

Most of the artists whose carvings and prints have so thrilled southerners over the last two and a half decades, lived, until recently, essentially the same kind of camp life that their ancestors knew for hundreds of years before them. There were some differences, of course. Most hunters killed with a gun, not bows and arrows; most Inuit gained part of their livelihood from trapping, and traded fur bales for the white man's goods.

In this century most Inuit are Christian, although Shamanism, the ancient religion of the hunting and gathering cultures whereby the world is ruled by spirit forces, still echoes in their lives. More than one shaman, the intermediary between the spirit forces and the community, has drawn his spirit helpers and put down his vision of the spirit world on paper. The shamanic content in some of the great prints undoubtedly represents the most eloquent statement of traditional Inuit belief since Knud Rasmussen, the fluently bilingual Greenlander of Inuit descent, published accounts of his talks with the Inuit collected during his 1921-24 journey across Arctic America.

Certainly there is much to interest the anthropologist and students of different cultures in Inuit sculpture and graphics. But perhaps there is more for the students of art.

It is not possible to miss the enormous vigour, the sure design, the elegance of form and execution which characterize Inuit art at its best. At the same time, it is probably too soon for concensus to identify without possibility of error, the most important works and artists. For instance, the early prints from Povungnituk, sadly neglected at the time of their release, are only now beginning to receive the attention they deserve. But while much sorting out waits to be done — massive amounts of Inuit art have reached the south — the universality of work commands our attention. One feels this, I think, in *Our Camp*, 1974 — Pitseolak's lyrical print of the Inuit family asleep in the safety of their tent; one senses it too, in some of the strongly dramatic Baker Lake prints of Simon Tookoome. Graphics like *A Time of Plenty*, 1971, *A Vision of Animals*, 1973, though uniquely Inuit in viewpoint, evoke celebration of the interrelatedness of life and man's place in the animal kingdom. Here, in the south, far from the hunting fields, they remind us that man is a mammal.

What is the history of Inuit art? The Inuit people first arrived in Arctic America several thousand years ago. They showed throughout the successive Inuit cultures that flourished on this continent, skill and craftsmanship in the manufacture of their tools and clothing. In addition, museums show us fine small carvings that may have had magical and religious significance. Later, in the 19th century, missionaries and anthropologists provided pencils and paper for drawing. Whalers and later the first traders were a market for ivory carvings.

Through the World War II years and immediately after, casual carving for the white man continued. Then in the late 1940s, the incident occurred which sparked the explosion of creativity that produced the sculpture and graphics now familiar to people around the world. The writer and artist James Houston, known to Inuit people as 'Sowmik', brought back small Inuit stone carvings from a sketching trip he made to Port Harrison in Arctic Quebec. Subsequently, a program to sponsor development of art in the North began. It was widely recognized that the Inuit needed a new source of income. The forces of change, sweeping in on Inuit life during the first fifty years of the century, were proceeding with terrifying rapidity. For the first time, as Inuit people put it, they had to "live with money." Out of this necessity has come an art of unexpected and remarkable quality.

The first contemporary sculpture to reach the south was followed by carvings from Baffin Island and by work from the western side of Hudson Bay. Print-making experiments began in Cape Dorset in 1957, and today five communities send yearly editions of prints south. Both carvings and prints from the various Arctic communities tend to have distinctive styles recognizable to the practiced eye.

Houston's journeys resulted in the start of many artistic careers. In Cape Dorset his first visit there is remembered as an event of very great importance.

"I remember when Sowmik came to Cape Dorset and asked for carvings", the old man Noah told me one day. "Everyone was carving. Kiakshuk made a special snow shelter to do the work. I never saw Niviaksee carve, but later I heard he was really good at it. Sometimes Sowmik liked my carvings; sometimes he gave them back to me. But once he told my son, Napatchee, 'that's very good', and he gave him a .22".

The artist Lucy recalls, "We would draw our art down there in camp and when a dog team went to get supplies from Cape Dorset, we would take along these drawings and give them to Sowmik. Then we'd go back and do some more".

What does the future hold? This is a question that is often asked nowadays. Only a handful of Inuit live full time on the land today. Since the middle 60s, settlements have effectively replaced camps, prefabs have replaced igloos, and all over the arctic children go to school. The Inuit people still like to be out on the land and many go whenever they can, especially in summer. However, the "old way" as the Inuit say, retreats now as the people who remember die. The content of the carving and prints is changing, faster in some communities than in others, and will continue to do so. There is great talent among young Inuit people, but how they will employ it in the future, is a question that cannot be answered today. All we know for the moment is that the Inuit who knew and lived the old life have had the great ability to create out of their lives a magnificent record — a record we know instinctively, as Pitseolak says, is "really true".

Levi Qumaluk
Walrus-Man-Boy.
41.8 x 47.5 x 25.0 cr
1975.69.1

Artist Unknown
Snow Goose. c. 1951
3.1 x 4.4 x 2.2 cm.
1975.65.2

A. Anaituq
Animals. 1975
2.6 x 7.3 x 16.2 cm.
1975.20.2

Tiyeatsian
Kayak and Seal in Bay. 1975
2.6 x 7.3 x 16.2 cm.
1975.20.3

A. Anaituq
Polar Bear and Owl. 1975
3.7 x 9.9 x 5.4 cm.
1975.20.1

Aquggaaq
Mother and Child.
25.0 x 26.5 x 33.0 cm.
1981.105.3

Kiawak
Smiling Family. 1966
32.5 x 48.5 x 17.5 cm.
1975.69.2

Henry
Bears and Seal.
19.0 x 16.5 x 13.0 cm.
1981.106.8

Peter Anautuk
Woman Nursing Child.
56.5 x 45.0 x 42.7 cm.
1981.98.4

149

Angrnasungaak
Musk-Ox. c. 1974
30.0 x 49.0 x 20.0 cm
1981.105.2

Davidee
Boot-Stretcher.
40.5 x 17.0 x 25.5 cm.
1975.20.4

Parr/Iyola
The Hunters. 1962
74.0 x 53.0 cm.
1975.37.2

Barnabas Akkanarshook
Mother and Three Children.
28.0 x 45.0 x 20.0 cm.
1975.25

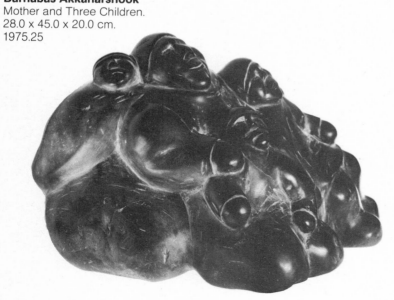

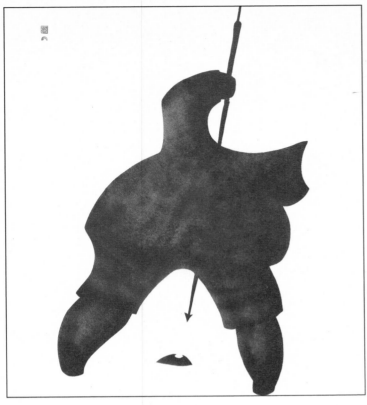

Niviaksiak
Man Hunting at a Seal Hole. 1959
59.7 x 44.6 cm.
1973.9

Kenojuak
Woman in the Sun. 1960
49.3 x 65.4 cm.
1975.65.1

Kananginak
Umingmuk. 1973
58.0 x 78.3 cm. (sight)
1981.93.9

Pitseolak
Our Camp. 1974
72.8 x 57.6 cm. (sight)
1981.94.6

Artist Unknown
Tsimshian, Human Face Mask.
22.0 x 16.8 x 12.8 cm.
1969.28

ART OF THE PACIFIC NORTHWEST COAST INDIAN

The Canadian art form best known to the rest of the world is that of our West Coast Indians. For almost a century, it has been rated internationally as one of the richest and most powerful of all tribal arts. As early as the late eighteenth century, Haida and Kwakiutl artifacts were finding their way into European collections.

Great forests provided the media for the majority of the Pacific northwest Indian artifacts. Cedar, fir and hemlock trees were transformed into masks, boats, totems, dwellings, utensils and clothes. The coastline supplied the sites for their villages, and the sea, generous provisions of food. Such a fortunate combination of circumstances enabled the coastal tribes to avoid the hazardous trips of their inland brothers and furnished ample leisure for lavish displays of boldly carved, decorated artifacts.

Their cultural area includes the entire coastline of British Columbia. The extreme generosity of the environment and the almost mystical atmosphere of the shrouded coast probably influenced the social and religious complexities which evolved with the first inhabitants. Supernatural creatures were basic to their concept of origin. The people created an art form which celebrated and communicated this belief while illustrating their lineal descent and providing a visual reminder of acquired privileges or rights. Status or prestige within the group was reinforced through the display of carved and painted paraphernalia.

The "potlatch" was the occasion for display when the dancers performed the origin myths wearing masks and costumes. Every conceivable object from small horn spoons to carved poles bore the totems or crests of the clan giving the feast. Generous gifts were given and if accepted, the guest recognized the ancestral and social claims of the giver whose nobility and status were thus enhanced.

Eight major tribal groups located along the coast are represented in The McMichael Canadian Collection. The Salish work differed significantly from that of the northern groups in artistic theme and style. The art was reflected in the costumes and adornments worn by the dancers to celebrate the guardian spirit myth.

The "Swaixwe" mask exemplifies the uniqueness of Coast Salish art with distinctive characteristics; bulging cylindrical eyes protrude as does the bulbous nose. Two birdhead horns surmount the head and backward pointing wooden spines are prominent on the splendid "Swaixwe" mask exhibited in The Collection.

The Nootka shared the northern belief that they were direct descendants of supernatural beings and claimed heraldic crests. Their decoration, in bold orange, blue and black, was often geometric and individual. The Nootka mask in The McMichael Collection, circa 1890, exhibits a downturned mouth.

The Kwakiutl perpetuated a complex system of secret societies each believed to have a mythical founder. In rituals and ceremonies dramatized during the winter months, dancers displayed large and complex masks often with movable parts which might reveal a mask face within. This dramatization of the idea of transformation was strengthened by the apparent possession of the dancers by supernaturals.

The "Hamatsa" or cannibal society was of major importance. The bird monsters "Hokhokw" (cracks open human skulls), "Kwakwakwalanooksiwae" (raven at the mouth of the river), and "Galodwudzuwis" (crooked beak of heaven), made their spectacular appearance as giant associates of the cannibal spirit. A fine Kwakiutl "Hamatsa" mask with a movable mouth may be seen in the gallery collection.

The Bella Coola were Salish migrants to the central coast of British Columbia. Their artists were motivated by a vision of the supernatural which was different from their neighbours', yet their masks rivalled those of the Kwakiutl. The dramatic carving of the Bella Coola is uniquely characterized by bulging features, heavy lines and a forceful use of colour, particularly a bright blue.

The McMichael Collection includes several Bella Coola masterpieces. The magnificent Bella Coola headdress figured prominently in ceremonies of the "Sisaok" society. A member was entitled to wear one or more weasel skins, and the nine skins on The Collection's headdress indicate the importance of the wearer. The "Sisaok" headdress is surmounted by upturned grizzly bear claws and has abalone insets.

North of the Bella Coolas was a group of Kwakiutl people known as the Bella Bella. Their artistic style was a fine mix whereby influences of the dramatic south were balanced by northern refinements. Bella Bella art is considered, by some, to be the most exciting of the entire coast. The Collection's two Bella Bella face masks are circa 1890.

Tribes of the Tsimshian are distributed along the river valleys of the Skeena and Nass. A zenith in superbly carved frontal headdresses and portrait masks was achieved. The face, either human or animal, was often framed by minute, detailed faces or animals. Large spaces were left unpainted and colour, when used, was subtle.

The Queen Charlotte Islands and the southern tip of Alaska's Prince of Wales Island were the homeland regions of the Haida. Like the Tsimshian, sparing use was made of colour, but the scale of their poles was more monumental. Superb Haida human portrait masks were created, and a magnificent example in The McMichael Collection is Charles Edensaw's "Old Lady Wearing Labrette", circa 1880. The delicate movable eyelids are controlled by concealed strings.

Argillite carvings of miniature totem poles, human figure replicas, pipes and spoons are universally recognized Haida artifacts. Nineteenth-century Haidas carved their familiar forms in argillite for trade goods. Decades later, splendid examples of this medium as an art form enhance The Collection, including the Raven Rattle, c. 1825.

The greatest of the Haida carvers, Charles Edensaw (1839-1924), is represented in The Collection by an exquisite bracelet, beaten and carved from silver dollars, and by his beautiful argillite carvings. Each of his works is a masterpiece in concept and design.

West Coast Indian art was both religious and social. The giant totem poles were heraldic crests in which each chief boasted of his strengths and privileges. These were made visual by the use of such symbols as the beaver, bear, frog and killer whale. Of the many thousands of majestic poles commissioned by the chiefs for their villages, most have now decayed — victims of neglect, combined with time and weather. The splendid Willie Seaweed pole from Blunden Harbour was the last standing pole on the island, long deserted by the Kwakiutl people, following a change in their fishing patterns.

Not long ago, it seemed that the traditional art of the coast peoples might not survive. Cultural confrontation and direct suppression of the "potlatch" custom by federal authorities were profound obstacles. Perseverance, personified by the efforts of the late Mungo Martin has led to a renewal of interest in this important facet of our cultural inheritance. Today there are growing numbers of fine artists who have schooled themselves in the coastal art tradition.

Doug Cranmer exhibits the strengths of his native heritage in his dramatically carved and painted lintels in the Western Canada gallery, together with his splendid adze-carved bench of British Columbia red cedar. Masterpieces like the gold box by the great Haida artist, Bill Reid, are contemporary and competently rival the art of old.

Artist Unknown
Bella Coola Sisaok Head-dress. 1924
54.0 x 31.5 x 38.0 cm.
1973.16.1

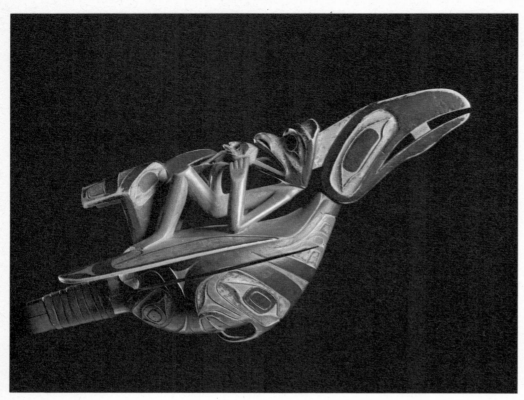

Artist Unknown
Haida Raven Rattle. c. 1825
11.0 x 31.7 x 10.3 cm.
1974.6

Willie Seaweed
Kwakiutl Totem Pole.
65.0 x 43.0 x 36.0 cm.
1970.19

The figures from the top down
Grizzly Bear
Thunderbird
Raven
Tsonoqua
Wasco

Artist Unknown
Bella Coola Thunderbird Mask. c. 1880
32.5 x 32.3 x 28.8 cm.
1981.104

Artist Unknown
(Kwakiutl) Komokwa Mask.
41.5 x 47.5 x 24.0 cm.
1977.2.2

Artist Unknown
Haida Figure. c. 1800s
21.7 x 5.8 x 6.5 cm.
1970.5.5

Artist Unknown
Haida Pipe. c. 1875
21.5 x 6.7 x 2.0 cm.
1977.5

Artist Unknown
Crooked Beak of the Sky Mask. c. 1880
29.0 x 20.3 x 86.0 cm.
1977.2.3

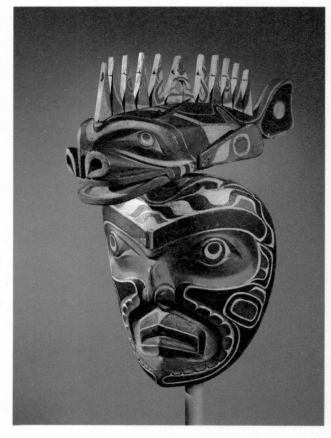

Artist Unknown
(Kwakiutl) Komokwa Mask.
66.0 x 35.5 x 62.0 cm.
1977.2.1

Charles Edensaw
Haida Bracelet. c. 1910
6.2 x 6.0 x 5.0 cm.
1981.108.1

Charles Edensaw
Totem Pole.
16.5 x 3.4 x 4.6 cm.
1977.29.2

Charles Edensaw
Gold Bracelet. c. 1899
1.5 x 8.6 x 5.8 cm.
1977.21

Charles Edensaw
Totem Pole.
16.4 x 3.4 x 3.0 cm.
1970.5.9

Charles Edensaw
Totem Pole.
11.0 x 3.7 x 4.1 cm.
1970.5.14

Norval Morrisseau
Artist's Wife and Daughter. 1975
101.6 x 81.3 cm.
1981.87.1

WOODLAND INDIAN ART

Woodland Indian contemporary art takes us into a world where a people preserves and perpetuates ancient crafts, tells us of its legends and of its dreams, lets us share the diverse expressions of its view of the world, and proves the continuing vigour of its creative power. Since ancient times, everyday functional objects of the Woodland Indians have been shaped with a keen sense of beauty. Tools, canoes and clothing were decorated; porcupine quills were dyed and applied to hide and birchbark; birchbark was embellished with scraped patterns, and wood was carved with a superb sense of design. The objects of the spiritual life were even more lovingly designed. The secrets of Midéwewin society were recorded in drawings, often stylized, which transmitted myth and sacred practices from generation to generation. The medicine masks of the Iroquois were a renewed challenge to successive generations to express dream and tradition.

Early contact with settlers introduced new designs and brought trade goods which modified old methods of decorating. Glass beads were used for splendid and gloriously colourful geometric patterns which complemented and, to some extent, replaced porcupine quill decorations. Many of the traditional art forms are carried on to the present day. Contemporary descendants of Woodland Indians have revived some lost crafts and have taken them far beyond the original traditional limits. This is exemplified by the Mohawk pottery of Oliver and Elda Smith of Hagersville, who rediscovered the techniques and materials of this ancient art. There, the pottery wheel was, at first, the only western addition to the ancient practice.

Through contact with the Europeans, silver and silver work was introduced to the Iroquois craftsmen, but by the middle of our century, this art had declined and the tradition of craftsmanship had almost disappeared. Again, a contemporary generation of craftsmen returned to tribal design, and artists, like Elwood Green, reached new heights of achievement.

The medicine masks of the Iroquois are among the works which have been consistently maintained. Fine carvings by J. Thomas and T. Harris exemplify the work of two generations of Iroquois carvers. These masks should be seen in terms of the encounter between the creator and the headman of the false faces.

The creator met the giant false face leader who claimed that he was the maker of the earth. The creator challenged him to a contest — who could move the mountain? The great false face shook his turtle rattle and summoned the mountain, but the mountain moved only slightly. When the creator gave the command, the mountain obeyed and enormous heat was generated. The great false face turned his head. His face struck the mountain, breaking his nose, and his mouth became distorted by pain. As the heat of the mountain threatened to suffocate him, he struggled for air and his tongue was drooping. The creator told the great false face that he would give him a place in the rocky hills of the west, near the rim of the earth. He assigned him to the tasks of blowing sweet gentle air over the crops, driving disease from the earth and assisting hunters and travellers.

In the last decade, a new sculptural medium, a brown stone, steatite, has been introduced by Duffy Wilson, an Iroquois (Tuscarora). In his masterful hands, it tells us of the history and legends of the Iroquois Federation. Younger artists in Oshwekin have used this new medium to advantage.

In the 1960s, an entirely new artistic development occurred in northern Ontario. Norval Morrisseau, born at Fort William, began to paint the legends of his people. He first used black ink on brown paper, depicting the spirits and their interaction with man. Later, the subject widened into images which dealt not only with myth, but also with his view of the prehistory of his people, the relation between man and fellow man, the place of man in nature, and his feelings about life. As the content of his paintings diversified, the use of colour became freer and a more important component of his composition. In the earliest works, tones of brown and green were used, but later, colours became bold, reminding us of stained glass windows or brilliantly coloured glass bead designs. The first attempts of Morrisseau to paint the sacred legends of his people were fiercely resisted by those who guarded the secrets of the Midéwewin society. However, Morrisseau persisted and as he developed his own capacity as a painter, the opposition to his work gradually declined. His influence on other native artists soon made itself felt.

Carl Ray, originally discouraged by the hostility which his drawings evoked among the leaders of his band at Sandy Lake, returned to his creative work and began to draw and paint his version of legends and of life. Ray developed into one of the most accomplished of Ontario's native graphic artists. Others of the same generation painted with a strong awareness of European schools of painting. Daphne Odjig had sketched as a child and had been imbued by her grandfather with the traditions of her people. She had travelled abroad and had finally synthesized a style and an approach which straddles two worlds, leaving her equally at home in both. Further south at Rama, Arthur Shilling had started to master impressionistic techniques and depict the faces of his people. He spent a brief period at the Ontario College of Art and although his technique is Western, Shilling's painting is Indian because he is Indian and deeply feels for his people.

The work of Morrisseau, Ray and others, began to exercise an influence all over northern Ontario. Young artists were inspired by the boldness with which the Indian spiritual heritage was set down. They began to find their own way and their own development within this framework. Saul Williams, of Round Lake, Roy Thomas of Long Lac, Joshim and Goyce Kakegamic of Red Lake, Benjamin Chee Chee of Temagami, and Sam Ashe of Pickle Lake were among those who developed their own creative personality and their own individualistic style. As their work developed, a distinctive school of Cree-Ojibwa-Odawa painting became discernible.

Further south on Manitoulin Island, the birthplace of Daphne Odjig and Francis Kagige, a group of young painters, still in high school, began to express themselves in drawings and paintings. Their artistic activities were a facet of their growing interest in their heritage, an aspect of self-discovery and a determination to preserve and recapture the essence of their Indian heritage. Foremost among them were Blake Debassige and Martin Panamick; the former working with bold, broad and visionary shapes, the latter with precise draughtsmanship and a love of nature. James Simon blends dream and reality and invents an imagery of animals and spirits. These three often paint with Randolph Trudeau and John LaFord, forming a group which bodes well for the future of Ontario native painting.

In parallel with the growth of the Cree-Ojibwa-Odawa school, there developed a group of painters whose art blended modern western artistic discoveries with Indian heritage. Odjig and Shilling are two of those artists. Others include Alex Janvier, who invents imaginary maps of pure colours which are graceful abstractions, and Clifford Maracle who uses the techniques of the Fauves to tell us what it is like to be an Indian in this technological world.

As we stand in the Woodland Indian gallery, we are enraptured by colour and form. We see the ancient traditions of the Woodland Indians preserved by contemporary native artists, re-expressed by a second self-taught group, who has invented new forms of artistic communication, and by a third group who uses modern western art. They are artists with enormous vigour and creative power and we are richer for having brought them together.

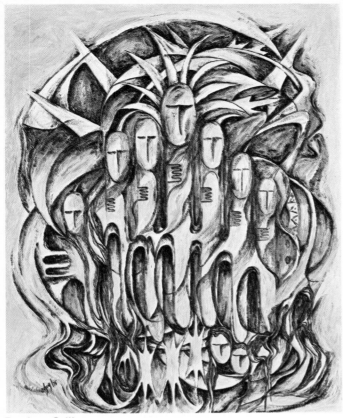

Daphne Odjig
Tribute to the Great Chiefs of the Past. 1975
101.8 x 81.0 cm.
1975.11.1

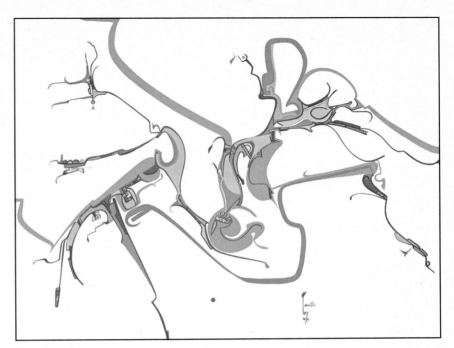

Alex Janvier
The Bureaucratic Supremist. 1975
56.0 x 71.3 cm.
1975.26.2

Clifford Maracle
Blue Indian Thinking. 1975
122.1 x 122.1 cm.
1975.42

Arthur Shilling
Self-portrait. c. 1975
84.0 x 61.4 cm.
1975.33.1

163

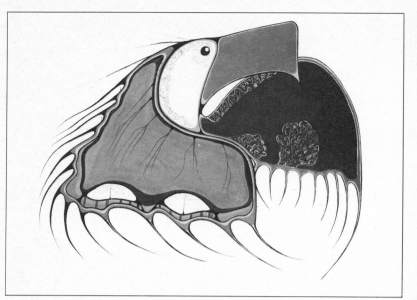

James Simon
Thunderer Spirit. 1975
76.0 x 91.3 cm.
1975.40.2

Norval Morrisseau
Sacred Mide Bear and Loon Totem. 1975
76.3 x 101.5 cm.
1975.38.1

Carl Ray
Frolicking Loons. 1975
55.9 x 76.2 cm.
1975.3.5

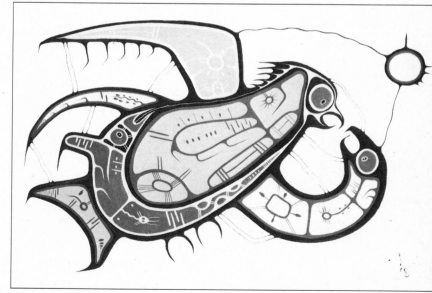

Roy Thomas
Thunderbird, Demon Fish, Light
56.0 x 84.0 cm.
1975.40.5

Duffy Wilson
To do da ho. 1975
14.0 x 19.5 x 11.0 cm.
1975.51

Elwood L. Green
Stone and Silver Sculpture. 1975
6.5 x 12.0 x 12.0 cm.
1975.48

Isabell Skye
Eagle Dancer Doll. c. 1975
51.5 x 84.0 x 29.0 cm.
1975.60

Jacob E. Thomas
Broken Nose Mask. c. 1975
77.0 x 28.0 x 12.8 cm.
1975.57.1

Joseph R. Jacobs
The Legend of the Crystal Bear. 1972
25.7 x 21.5 x 28.2 cm.
1975.55